Lift Up Your Hearts

Songs for Creative Worship

Linda White, editor

Pew Edition

Geneva Press
Louisville, Kentucky

Cover design by Pam Poll

First edition
Published by Geneva Press
Louisville, Kentucky

This book is printed on acid free paper that meets the American National Standards Institute Z39.48 standard. ∞

PRINTED IN THE UNITED STATES OF AMERICA
99 00 01 02 03 04 05 06 07 08 — 10 9 8 7 6 5 4 3 2 1

ISBN 0-664-50030-7 (Leader's Edition)
ISBN 0-664-50029-3 (Presbyterian Pew Edition)
ISBN 0-664-50144-3 (Ecumenical Pew Edition)

Contents

Foreword

Let us lift up our hearts as well
as our hands
to God in heaven.
Lam. 3:41

Lift Up Your Hearts, a collection of contemporary songs and hymns for use in Christian worship, appears at a time of great flux in the life and liturgy of the church. People today are hungry for experiences of the holy, but established patterns of church attendance, Christian education, and liturgical practice are undergoing great change. People come to churches seeking spiritual meaning and depth, but they often have little acquaintance with the church's vocabulary, the biblical story, the great hymns of the tradition, and the classical language of worship.

In response to this new cultural climate, many congregations have been experimenting with newer styles of worship, including contemporary music that is easy to learn and to sing. Sometimes tensions have arisen in congregations as older, more traditional worship forms jostled with the newer, less formal styles. As more and more churches have adapted their worship patterns, the need has arisen for a collection of songs and hymns that would, on the other hand, embody the strong theology and musical excellence vital to trustworthy Christian liturgy. *Lift Up Your Hearts* is addressed to this need.

The committee that assembled the collection of songs in *Lift Up Your Hearts* has sought, in every case, to find music that faithfully expresses the convictions of the Reformed theological tradition. A wide variety of contemporary Christian music was surveyed in order to select the best songs for this collection. Whenever possible and needed, changes have been made in the language of the songs to render them inclusive in regard to language about human beings. All of the music is easy to sing, but not simplistic or overly sentimental.

There are two versions of *Lift Up Your Hearts:* the Leader's Edition and the Pew Edition. The Leader's Edition is a large-format book featuring written-out accompaniment for all songs, including parts for various instruments where suitable, as well as suggestions for tempo and interpretation. The Pew Edition is a smaller, easy-to-hold book, which includes the words, melody line, and guitar chords of the songs. This edition is available in two different bindings, designated Presbyterian Pew Edition and Ecumenical Pew Edition.

We hope that these songs will bless you and your congregation as they have blessed those of us who have assembled this collection. Our prayer is that, as you sing these songs, you will truly be encouraged to "lift up your hearts" to God.

Linda White, Editor

As We Gather in This Place

Gathering

Words and music by
Kevin Boyd

As we gath-er in this place We have come to seek your face. May our lives re-flect your grace As we gath-er in this place.

Blessed Are Those

Ps. 84
Gathering

Words and Music by
Burns Stanfield

Bless-ed are those who dwell in your house, Ev-er sing-ing your praise. Bless-ed are those who dwell in your house, Ev-er sing-ing your praise.

1. AS WE GATHER IN THIS PLACE   2. BLESSED ARE THOSE

City of God

Isa. 40:1–9
Gathering

Words and Music by
Dan Schutte

1. A - wake from your slum - ber!
2. We are sons of the morn - ing;
3. O __ com - fort my peo - ple;

A - rise from your sleep! A new day is
we are daugh-ters of day. The one who has
make gen - tle your words. Pro-claim to my

dawn - ing for all those who weep.
loved us has bright-ened our way.
cit - y the day of her birth.

The peo - ple in dark - ness have seen a great
The Lord of all kind - ness has called us to
O cit - y of glad - ness, now lift up your

Light. The Lord of our long - ing
be A light for his peo - ple
voice. Pro - claim the good tid - ings

has con-quered the night.
to set their hearts free.
that all may re - joice.

Let us

3. CITY OF GOD

Come and Fill

Gathering

Words and Music by
The Taizé Community

Family Song

John 3:31–35
Gathering/Community

Words and Music by
Steve Hampton

Here we are, gath - ered to - geth-
(sing - ing)

- er as a fam - i - ly;

Bound as one, lift - ing up our voic - es to the

King of kings. We cry, "Ab - ba,
(We sing,)

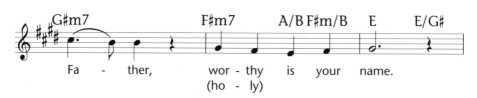

Fa - ther, wor - thy is your name.
(ho - ly)

Ab - ba, Fa - ther, wor - thy is your name."
(ho - ly)

5. **FAMILY SONG**

I Was Glad

Ps. 122:1
Gathering

Words and Music by
Kinley Lange

I Will Call upon the Lord

Ps. 18:3, 46
Gathering

Words and Music by
Michael O'Shields

I will call up-on the Lord

who is wor-thy to be praised.

So shall I be saved from my en-e-mies. _____

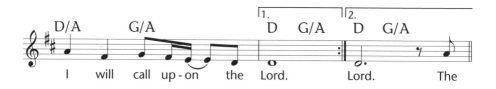

I will call up-on the Lord. Lord. The

Lord liv-eth, and bless-ed be the Rock. And let the God

_____ of my sal-va-tion be ex-alt-ed. The Lord liv-eth, and

7. I WILL CALL UPON THE LORD

bless - ed   be   the   Rock,   and   let   the   God __   of   my   sal -

va-tion be ex - alt   -   ed.   The   ed.

Optional Descant

Verse

I   will   call   up-on   the   Lord

who   is   wor - thy   to   be   praised.

So   shall   I   be   saved   from   my   en - e - mies.

Second time to Chorus

I   will   call   up - on   the   Lord.

7.   I WILL CALL UPON THE LORD

Come into His Presence

Rom. 10:9; Rev. 5:12
Gathering

Composer/Lyricist: Unknown

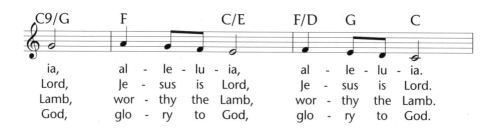

1. Come in - to his pres-ence sing - ing Al - le - lu -
2. Come in - to his pres-ence sing - ing Je - sus is
3. Praise the Lord to - geth - er sing - ing Wor - thy the
4. Praise the Lord to - geth - er sing - ing Glo - ry to

ia, al - le - lu - ia, al - le - lu - ia.
Lord, Je - sus is Lord, Je - sus is Lord.
Lamb, wor - thy the Lamb, wor - thy the Lamb.
God, glo - ry to God, glo - ry to God.

Come in - to his pres - ence sing - ing Al - le - lu -
Come in - to his pres - ence sing - ing Je - sus is
Praise the Lord to - geth - er sing - ing Wor - thy the
Praise the Lord to - geth - er sing - ing Glo - ry to

Last time, repeat as necessary

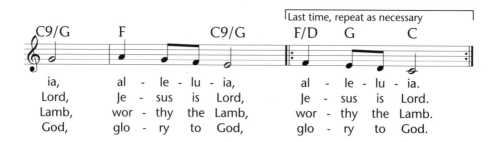

ia, al - le - lu - ia, al - le - lu - ia.
Lord, Je - sus is Lord, Je - sus is Lord.
Lamb, wor - thy the Lamb, wor - thy the Lamb.
God, glo - ry to God, glo - ry to God.

Jesus, We Are Here

Gathering

Words and Music by
Patrick Matsikenyiri

Je - sus,   we are here,   Je - sus,
Je - su   ta - wa   pa - no,   Je - su

we are here,   Je - sus,   we are here,
ta - wa   pa - no,   Je - su   ta - wa   pa - no,

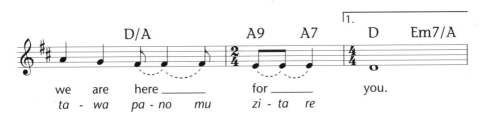

we are here _____ for _____ you.
ta - wa   pa - no   mu   zi - ta   re

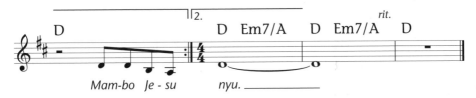

Mam - bo Je - su   nyu. _____

Let Us Go!

Ps. 100:2, 4; Ps. 122:1
Call to Worship

Words and Music by
Walt Harrah

1. I re - joiced with those who said to me,
(2. We have) come to lis - ten to the Word,
(3. He will) meet us as we seek his face,

"Let us go to the house of the Lord." There's no
Here the
And he

oth - er place I'd rath-er be,
Spir - it's pres-ence is as-sured. Let us go to the house of the Lord.
chang-es peo-ple in this place.

Gath-ered here with all God's fam - i - ly,
Je - sus Christ will be ex - alt - ed here, Let us
With a grate-ful heart we've come to sing,

Who could ask for bet - ter
go to the house of the Lord. As the one we wor-ship
Giv - ing thanks to God in

com-pa - ny?
and re - vere. Let us go to the house of the Lord.
ev - ery-thing.

En - ter in - to his gates with praise, Thank the Lord Most High.

___ En - ter in - to his courts with joy,

praise and glo - ri - fy. ____

⌐1., 2.

⌐3.

2. We have
3. He will

And glo - ri - fy. ____ And glo - ri - fy!

10. LET US GO!

Make a Joyful Noise

Ps. 100
Gathering

Words and Music by
Kinley Lange

Make a joy - ful noise un - to the Lord,

all peo - ple make a joy - ful noise. __

Last time to Coda

Make a joy - ful noise un - to the Lord, all

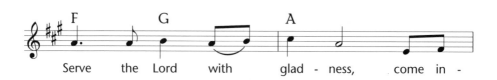

peo - ple make a joy - ful noise. __

Serve the Lord with glad - ness, come in -

to God's pres-ence with a song. Serve the Lord with

11. **MAKE A JOYFUL NOISE**

glad-ness, come in - to God's pres-ence with a song. Make a

✠ **Coda**

peo - ple make a joy - ful noise! __

11.   MAKE A JOYFUL NOISE

Make a Joyful Noise All the Earth

Ps. 100
Gathering

Words and Music by
Linnea Good

Make a joy-ful noise all the earth!

Wor-ship your God with glad-ness. Make a joy-ful noise all the earth.

Come to this place with a song!

Verses

1. Know that your God has made you.
2. En - ter these gates, thanks giv - ing.
3. A - ges through end - less a - ges,

Know it's to God we be - long. And
En - ter these courts ___ with praise. Sing
sea - sons of end - less years, the

come to this place with joy - ful-ness and praise.
thanks to your God and bless this ho - ly name.
love of our ma - ker ev - er shall en - dure.

Wor - ship your God with a song!

12. **MAKE A JOYFUL NOISE ALL THE EARTH**

Spirit Song

Col. 1:9–13
Gathering/Jesus the Son

Words and Music by
John Wimber

1. O let the Son of God en-fold you with his
2. O come and sing this song with glad-ness as your

Spir-it and his love, Let him fill your life and
hearts are filled with joy, Lift your hands in sweet sur-

sat-is-fy your soul. O let him
ren-der to his name. O give him

have the things that hold you and his Spir-it, like a
all your tears and sad-ness, give him all your years of

dove, Will des-cend up-on your life and make you
pain, And you'll en-ter in-to life in Je-sus'

whole. Je-sus, O Je-sus,
name.

come and fill your lambs. Je-sus, O

Je-sus, come and fill your lambs.

13. SPIRIT SONG

Over My Head

Traditional

1. O-ver my head I hear mu-sic in the air.
(2. O-ver my) head I hear sing-ing in the air.

O-ver my head I hear mu-sic in the air.
O-ver my head I hear sing-ing in the air.

O-ver my head I hear mu-sic in the air.
O-ver my head I hear sing-ing in the air.

There must be a God some-where. 2. O-ver my
There must be a God some -

where. There must be a God some-where.

This Is the Day

Ps. 118:24
Gathering

Words and Music by
Bobby Fisher

This is the day, — This is

the day, — This is the day — that the

Lord has made! Let us re-joice,

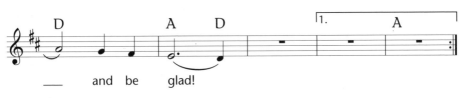

Let us re-joice, — Let us re-joice

— and be glad!

1.
2.
Let us re-joice — and be glad! —

15. THIS IS THE DAY

We Are the Family of God

Eph. 3:14–21
Gathering/Community

Words and Music by
Jon Byron

16. WE ARE THE FAMILY OF GOD

You Oh Lord Are a Great God

Heb. 13:15
Gathering

Words and Music by
Terry and Randy Butler

1. I come to you oh Lord _ with a
(2. I) bring to you oh Lord _ a

thank - ful heart.   I sing my song of love _
sac - ri - fice of praise. _   And of your won-drous works,

_ and praise for who you are. ___
_ I'll sing for all my days. ___

For you oh Lord are a great God,

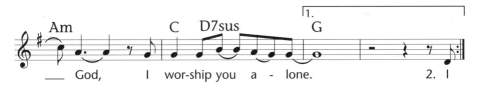

glo - ri - ous and strong.   You oh Lord are a great

___ God,   I wor-ship you a - lone.   2. I

For you oh Lord are a great __ God,

glo - ri - ous and strong. You oh Lord are a great

__ God, I wor-ship you a - lone. I

come to you oh Lord __ with a thank - ful heart.

17. YOU OH LORD ARE A GREAT GOD

You Are Here

Gathering

Words and Music by
Martin J. Nystrom and Don Moen

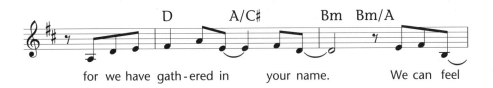

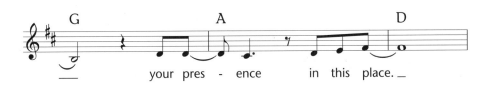

18. YOU ARE HERE

in our midst, how we've wait - ed for mo-

- ments like this. __ Have your way __ in this place,

__ Ho - ly Spir - it, come do as you wish.

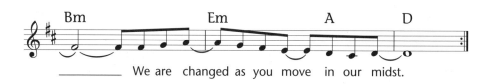

__ We are changed as you move in our midst.

18. **YOU ARE HERE**

Alleluia!

Songs of Praise

Words and Music by
Michael McCarty

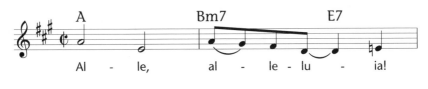

Al - le, al - le - lu - ia!

Al - le, al - le - lu - ia! Al - le,

al - le - lu - ia! Al - le, al - le - lu - ia!

19. ALLELUIA! (McCarty)

Alleluia

Songs of Praise

Words and Music by
Jerry Sinclair

20. **ALLELUIA (Sinclair)**

Alleluia, Thanks Be to God

Songs of Praise

Words and Music by
Jim Strathdee

Al - le - lu - ia, al - le - lu - ia, al - le - lu - ia, thanks be to God.

Descant—second time

Al - le - lu - ia, al - le - lu - ia, al - le - lu - ia, thanks be to God.

Blessed Be the Lord God Almighty

Rev. 4:8
Songs of Praise/Response to Pardon

Words and Music by
Bob Fitts

Fa - ther in heav-en, how we love you, we

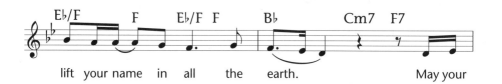

lift your name in all the earth. May your

king - dom be es-tab-lished in our prais - es,

as your peo - ple de - clare your might - y works.

Bless-ed be the Lord God Al - might - y, who

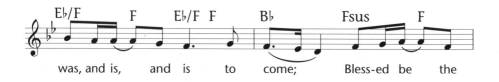

was, and is, and is to come; Bless-ed be the

22. BLESSED BE THE LORD GOD ALMIGHTY

22. **BLESSED BE THE LORD GOD ALMIGHTY**

Awesome God

Ps. 145:1–9; James 3:17
Songs of Praise

Words and music by
Rich Mullins

Our God is an awe - some God,

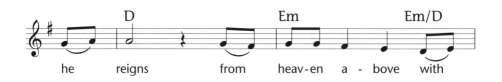

he reigns from heav-en a - bove with

wis - dom, pow'r and love. Our God is an awe-some

God! Our God! Our God is an awe - some

God! Our God is an awe-some God!

God Is So Good

2 Chron. 5:11–14
Songs of Praise

Words and Music: Unknown

1. God is so good,
2. God an - swers prayer,
3. God cares for me,
4. God, you're so good,

God is so good, God is so
God an - swers prayer, God an - swers
God cares for me, God cares for
God, you're so good, God, you're so

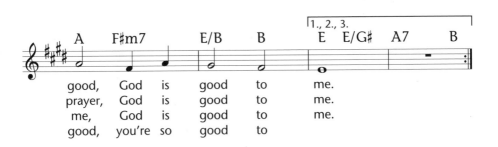

good, God is good to me.
prayer, God is good to me.
me, God is good to me.
good, you're so good to

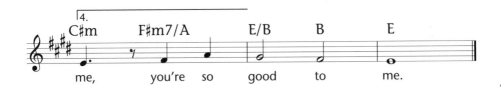

me, you're so good to me.

From the Sun's Rising

Matt. 28:16
Songs of Praise

Words and music by
Graham Kendrick

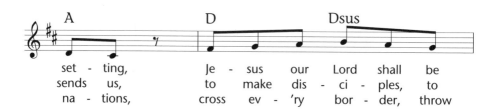
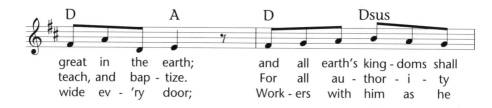

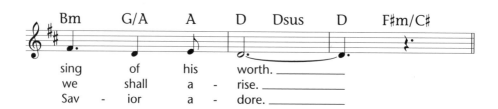

25. FROM THE SUN'S RISING

25. **FROM THE SUN'S RISING**

Blessed Be Your Holy Name

Songs of Praise

Words and Music by
Eddie Espinosa

26. BLESSED BE YOUR HOLY NAME

God the Creator

Psalm 37:5
Songs of Praise

Gaelic melody
Words and arrangement by
The Iona Community

1. God the Cre - a - tor, you in love made me,
2. O Christ the Sav - ior, you in love called me,

who once was noth - ing, but now have grown.
who once was no one, lost and a - lone.

I bring the best of all my life of - fers;
I pledge to go wher - ev - er you sum - mon,

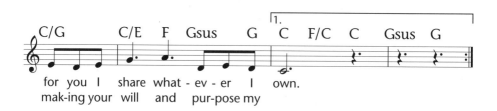

for you I share what - ev - er I own.
mak-ing your will and pur-pose my

own.   3. O God the spir - it, you in love
                        peo - ple sum-moned to -

27. **GOD THE CREATOR**

F	C				Am	F	C/E

move me,   who once was   no - where   and felt un -
geth - er   to be the   Church in   which faith is

B♭	G	C		C/E	F	C/G

known.   I know my   need of   you for com -
sown.   I make my   prom - ise   to live for

Am	D/F♯	C/G	Fmaj7	C/E	F	G

pan - ion: all things can   change when   not on my
Je - sus   and let the   world know   all are his

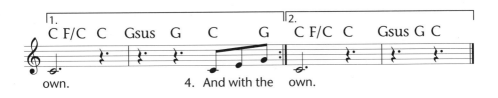

1.
C F/C	C	Gsus	G	C

2.
G	C F/C	C	Gsus G C

own.   4. And with the   own.

27. GOD THE CREATOR

Halle, Halle, Hallelujah

Songs of Praise

Music: Unknown
Arr. Geoff Weaver

Hal - le, hal - le, hal - le - lu -

jah! Hal - le, hal - le, hal - le -

lu - jah! Hal - le, hal - le, hal - le -

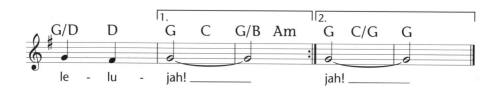

lu - jah! Hal - le - lu - jah, hal -

le - lu - jah! _____ jah! _____

28. HALLE, HALLE, HALLELUJAH

Great and Mighty

Ps. 150
Songs of Praise

Words and Music by
Marlene Bigley

29. GREAT AND MIGHTY

Great Is the Lord

Songs of Praise

Words and Music by
Michael W. Smith and Deborah D. Smith

1. Great is the Lord, he is ho-ly and just.
2. Great are you, Lord, You are ho-ly and just:

By his pow-er we trust in his love.
By your po-wer we trust in your love.

Great is the Lord, he is faith-ful and true;
Great are you, Lord, you are faith-ful and true;

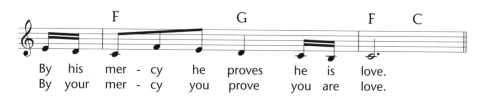

By his mer-cy he proves he is love.
By your mer-cy you prove you are love.

Great is the Lord, and wor-thy of glo-ry!
Great are you, Lord, and wor-thy of glo-ry!

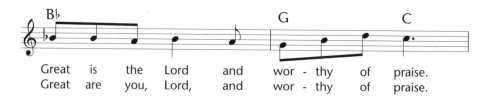

Great is the Lord and wor-thy of praise.
Great are you, Lord, and wor-thy of praise.

30. GREAT IS THE LORD

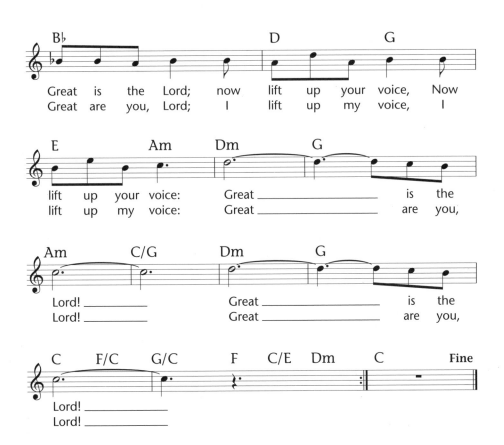

Great is the Lord; now lift up your voice, Now
Great are you, Lord; I lift up my voice, I

lift up your voice: Great _____ is the
lift up my voice: Great _____ are you,

Lord! _____ Great _____ is the
Lord! _____ Great _____ are you,

Lord! _____
Lord! _____

30. **GREAT IS THE LORD**

Holy Is the Lord on High

Songs of Praise

Words and Music by
Scott Brenner

In the still - ness of this hour __

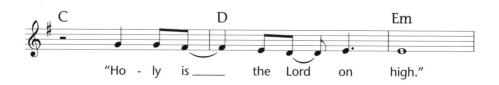

I wor - ship you, my Lord, __ cry - ing,

"Ho - ly is ____ the Lord on high."

In the qui - et of my heart __

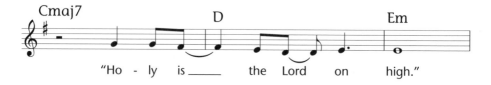

I sing this song of praise, cry - ing,

"Ho - ly is ____ the Lord on high."

31. HOLY IS THE LORD ON HIGH

And for all of my days ____ I will

bow down be - fore ____ you, giv-ing glo - ry and hon -

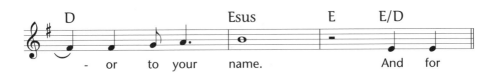
- or to your name. And for

all of my life ____ I will wor - ship and a - dore

____ you, cry-ing, "Ho - ly is ____ the Lord on

high." In the still - cry - ing,

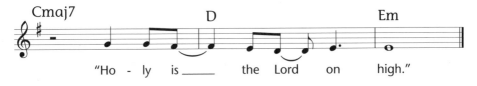
"Ho - ly is ____ the Lord on high."

31. HOLY IS THE LORD ON HIGH

Holy Lord

Isa. 6:3
Songs of Praise

Words and Music by
Claire Cloninger and Don Moen

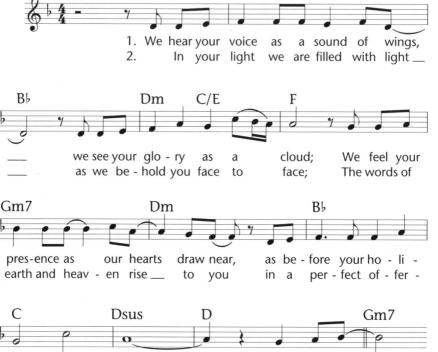

Tribes and tongues raise a song — like ho - ly

thun - der, _____ sing - ing, "Ho - ly, ho - ly, ho -

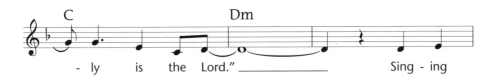

- ly is the Lord." _____ Sing - ing

"Ho - ly, ho - ly, ho - ly is the Lord. __

32. **HOLY LORD**

He Is Exalted

Songs of Praise/Christ the King/Transfiguration

Words and Music by
Twila Paris

How Can I Keep from Singing?

Ps. 30:5
Songs of Praise

Words and Music by Robert Lowry,
Bright Jewels for the Sunday School, 1869
Refrain music alt.

1. My life flows on in end - less song,
   a - bove earth's lam - en - ta - tion. I
   catch the sweet, though far - off hymn that
   hails a new cre - a - tion.

2. Through all the tu - mult and the strife,
   I hear that mus - ic ring - ing. It
   finds an ech - o in my soul. How
   can I keep from sing-ing?

3. What though my joys and com - forts die?
   The Lord my Sav - ior liv - eth. What
   though the dark - ness gath - er round? Songs
   in the night he giv - eth.

4. The peace of Christ makes fresh my heart,
   a foun - tain ev - er spring - ing! All
   things are mine since I am his! How
   can I keep from sing-ing?

Refrain

No storm can shake my in - most calm while to that Rock I'm cling - ing. Since love is Lord of heav'n and earth, how can I keep from sing-ing?

34.   HOW CAN I KEEP FROM SINGING?

I Sing Praises

Songs of Praise

Words and Music by
Terry MacAlmon

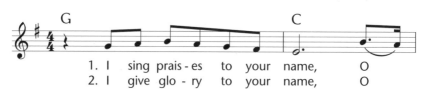

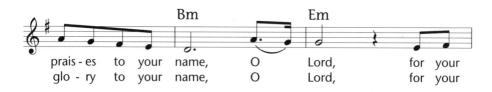

I Will Sing of the Mercies

Songs of Praise

Words and Music by
John Barnett

In the Presence of Your People

Ps. 22:3,22; Ps. 116:14
Response to Pardon/Songs of Praise

Words para. by Brent Chambers
Music by Brent Chambers

37. IN THE PRESENCE OF YOUR PEOPLE

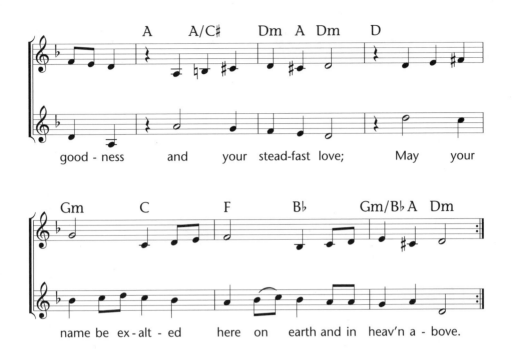

good - ness   and   your   stead-fast love;   May   your

name be ex - alt - ed   here   on   earth and in heav'n a - bove.

I Will Worship You, Lord

Ps. 72:19
Songs of Praise

Words and Music by
Daniel Gardner

38. I WILL WORSHIP YOU, LORD

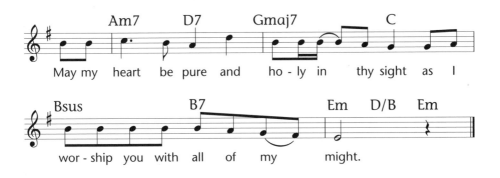

Am7   D7   Gmaj7   C

May my heart be pure and ho - ly in thy sight as I

Bsus   B7   Em   D/B   Em

wor - ship you with all of my might.

Jesus, Name above All Names

John 1:1–14
Songs of Praise/Advent

Words and Music by
Naida Hearn

F   Am

Je - sus, name a - bove all names;

Gm7

beau - ti - ful Sav - ior, glo - ri - ous

C   Bb/C   Am/C   C7   F

Lord. _____ Em - man - u - el,

Am

God is with us; bless - ed Re -

Gm7   C7   F

deem - er, Liv - ing Word. _____

Jesus, You're the Way

John 14:6
Songs of Praise

Words and Music by
Walt Harrah

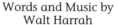

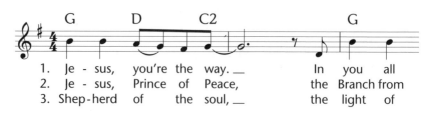

1. Je - sus, you're the way. __ In you all
2. Je - sus, Prince of Peace, the Branch from
3. Shep - herd of the soul, __ the light of

truth is found, The foun - tain - head of life, __
Da - vid's throne, Mes - si - ah Son of God,
ev - 'ry - one, __ the King of Kings who reigns

__ the on - ly door: _____
__ the Great I Am: _____
__ in glo - ry now: _____

Where else can I turn? _ Where else can I go?

__ You a - lone have the on - ly words I

40. JESUS, YOU'RE THE WAY

need to know.

You a - lone have the

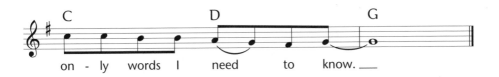

on - ly words I need to know. ___

40. JESUS, YOU'RE THE WAY

Let There Be Praise

Songs of Praise

Words and Music by
Melodie and Dick Tunney

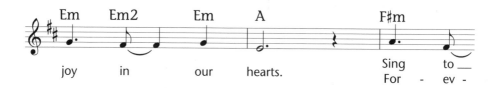

1., 2. Let there be praise, let there be

joy in our hearts. Sing to ___
For - ev -

the Lord, give him the glo - ry; ___
- er - more let his love

fill the air, and

let there be praise.

Let there be praise, let there be

41. LET THERE BE PRAISE

41. LET THERE BE PRAISE

Lord of All

Songs of Praise

Words and Music by
Danny Daniels

You are Lord o - ver night __ and day.

You are Lord and the one __ who saves. You are Lord and we sing

__ your praise. You are Lord of all. ____

You are Lord of the winds that blow. You are Lord in the love

__ you show. You are Lord; let the peo - ple know

You are Lord of all! ____ You are Lord

of the heav - ens. You are Lord __ of the na - tions.

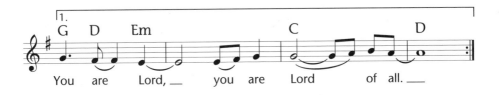

You   are   Lord, ___   you   are   Lord   of   all. ___

You   are   Lord, ___   you   are   Lord   of   all!

Lord, Be Glorified

Songs of Praise

Words and Music by
Bob Kilpatrick

In   my   life,   Lord,   be   glo - ri - fied,
In   your   church,   Lord,   be   glo - ri - fied,

be   glo - ri - fied.   In   my   life,   Lord,
be   glo - ri - fied.   In   your   church,   Lord,

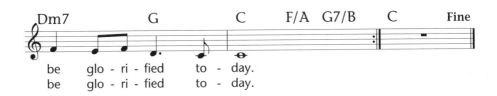

be   glo - ri - fied   to - day.
be   glo - ri - fied   to - day.

43.   LORD, BE GLORIFIED

Lord, Glorify Your Name

Songs of Praise

Words and Music by
Robert Hartmann

Lord, You Are the Holy One

Songs of Praise

Words and Music by
Lynn DeShazo

Lord, you are the Ho - ly One, and by your grace we come to sing this song to you, we de - light our - selves in you; For - ev - er you're the same, we mag - ni - fy your name, and of your deeds we tell, Ho - ly One of Is - ra - el. Lord, you are Ho - ly, ho - ly. And you are wor - thy to be praised; Fa - ther, we love you, love you. There is no oth - er who shall reign.

45. LORD, YOU ARE THE HOLY ONE

Majesty

Songs of Praise/Easter/Ascension/Christ the King

Words and Music by
Jack W. Hayford

Maj - es - ty, _____ wor-ship his maj - es - ty; _____

_____ un - to Je - sus be all glo - ry, hon-or and

praise. _____ Maj - es - ty, _____ king-dom au-

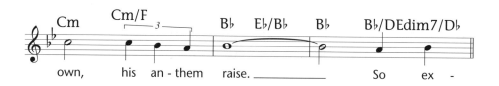

thor - i - ty _____ flow from his throne un - to his

own, his an - them raise. _____ So ex -

alt, lift up on high the name of Je - sus; _____

mag - ni - fy, come glo - ri - fy Christ Je - sus, the

King. Maj - es - ty, _____ wor-ship his

maj - es - ty; _____ Je - sus who died, now glo - ri -

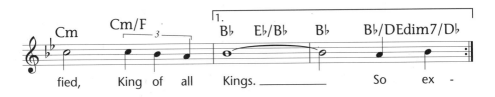
fied, King of all Kings. _____ So ex -

Kings. Je - sus, who died, now glo - ri -

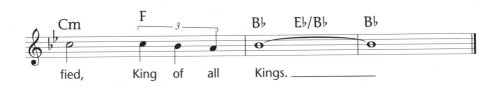
fied, King of all Kings. _____

46. MAJESTY

Santo, Santo

Songs of Praise

Words and Music: Unknown

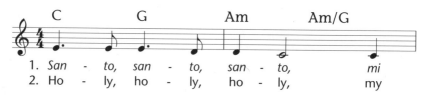

1. San - to, san - to, san - to, mi
2. Ho - ly, ho - ly, ho - ly, my

co - ra - zón te_a - do - ra! Mi co - ra - zón te
heart, my heart a - dores you! My heart is glad to

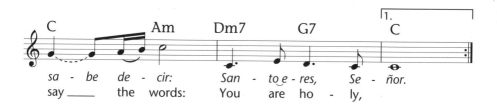

sa - be de - cir: San - to_e - res, Se - ñor.
say ___ the words: You are ho - ly,

Lord. You are ho - ly, Lord.

Music arrangement © 1993 Geoff Weaver/Jubilate Hymns.
Used by permission of G.I.A. Publications, Inc.

47. SANTO, SANTO

Praise, I Will Praise You, Lord

Ps. 145
Songs of Praise

Words and Music by
Claude Fraysse

1. Praise, I will praise you, Lord,
2. Love, I will love you, Lord, with
3. Serve, I will serve you, Lord,

all my heart. O God, I will tell the

won-ders of your ways, and glo-ri-fy your name.

Praise, I will praise you, Lord,
Love, I will love you, Lord, with all my
Serve, I will serve you, Lord

heart. In you I will find the source of all my joy.

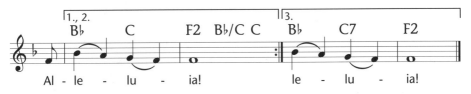

Al - le - lu - ia! le - lu - ia!

48. PRAISE, I WILL PRAISE YOU, LORD

Mighty Is Our God

Ps. 93:4
Songs of Praise

Words and Music by
Don Moen, Eugene Greco, and Gerrit Gustafson

Might-y is our God, might-y is our King;

Might-y is our Lord, —

rul-er of ev-'ry-thing. Glor-y to our God,

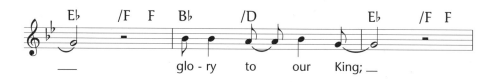

glo-ry to our King; —

Glo-ry to our Lord, rul-er of ev-'ry-thing.

His name is high - er, high-er than an - y oth-

49. MIGHTY IS OUR GOD

49. **MIGHTY IS OUR GOD**

Shine, Jesus, Shine

Songs of Praise

Words and Music by
Graham Kendrick

1. Lord, the light of your love is shin - ing
2. Lord, I come to your awe - some pres - ence,
3. As we gaze on your king - ly bright - ness,

in the midst of the dark - ness, shin - ing;
from the shad - ows in - to your ra - dience;
so our fa - ces dis - play your like - ness,

Je - sus, Light of the World, shine up - on us,
by the blood I may en - ter your bright - ness,
ev - er chang - ing from glo - ry to glo - ry,

set us free by the truth you now bring - us:
search me, try me, con - sume all my dark - ness:
mir - rored here may our lives tell your sto - ry:

Shine on me, shine on me.

50. SHINE, JESUS, SHINE

Shine, Je - sus, shine, _ fill this land with the

Fa - ther's glo - ry. Blaze, Spir - it, blaze, set our

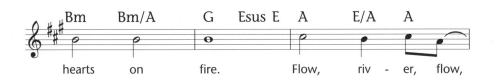

hearts on fire. Flow, riv - er, flow,

_ flood the na - tions with grace and mer - cy.

Send forth your word, _ Lord, and let there be

light! _____ light!

light! _____

50. SHINE, JESUS, SHINE

The Name of the Lord

Prov. 18:10
Songs of Praise

Music by
Clinton Utterbach

51. THE NAME OF THE LORD

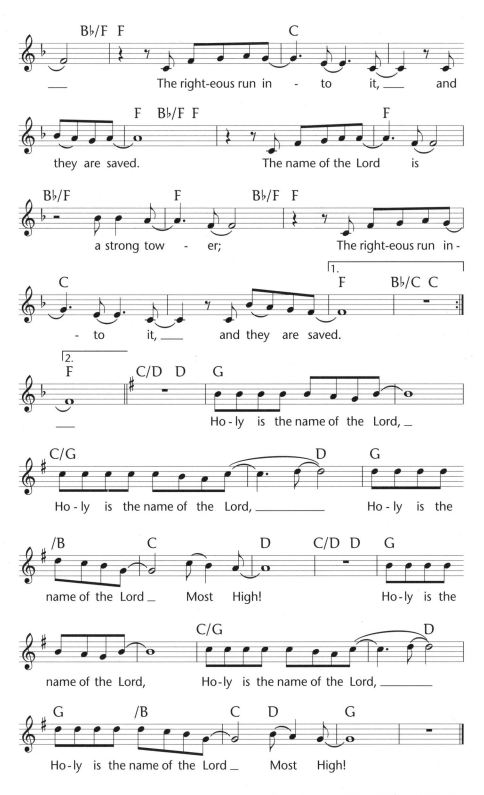

51. **THE NAME OF THE LORD**

Sing Hallelujah

Songs of Praise

Words and Music by
Linda Stassen

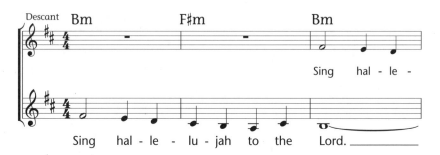

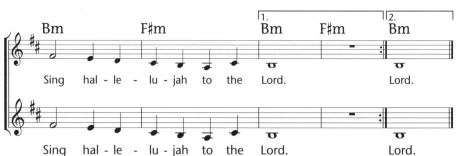

52. SING HALLELUJAH

Sing unto the Lord

Ps. 96:1, 4
Songs of Praise/Call to Worship/Psalm Refrain

Words and Music: Unknown
Arr. by Tom Fettke

53.   SING UNTO THE LORD

Thou Art Worthy

Rev. 4:11
Songs of Praise

Words and Music by
Pauline Michael Mills

54. THOU ART WORTHY

We Will Glorify

Songs of Praise

Words and Music by
Twila Paris

1. We will glo - ri - fy the King of kings, we will
2. Lord Je - ho - vah reigns in maj - es - ty, we will
3. He is Lord of heav - en, Lord of earth, he is
4. Hal - le - lu - jah to the King of kings, hal - le -

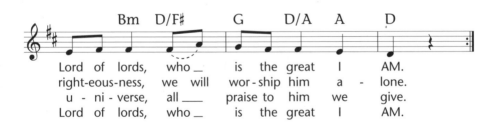

glo - ri - fy the Lamb; We will glo - ri - fy the
bow be - fore his throne; We will wor - ship him in
Lord of all who live; He is Lord a - bove the
lu - jah to the Lamb; Hal - le - lu - jah to the

Lord of lords, who __ is the great I AM.
right-eous-ness, we will wor - ship him a - lone.
u - ni - verse, all __ praise to him we give.
Lord of lords, who __ is the great I AM.

55. WE WILL GLORIFY

We Are Singing

Ps. 27:1–4; 96:1, 4; Col. 3:16
Songs of Praise

Zulu text and music based on the
South African freedom song "Siyahamba."
Free paraphrase of Zulu text in English, additional text,
and music arrangement by Hal H. Hopson

Refrain

We are sing - ing, for the Lord is our light,
See yah hahm buh koo kah nigh nee kwen kohs,

We are sing - ing, for the Lord is our light. ___
see yah hahm buh koo kah nigh nee kwen kohs. ___

We are sing - ing, for the Lord is our light,
See yah hahm buh koo kah nigh nee kwen kohs,

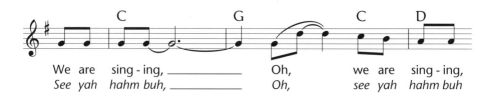

We are sing - ing, for the Lord is our light. ___
see yah hahm buh koo kah nigh nee kwen kohs. ___

We are sing - ing, _____ Oh, we are sing - ing,
See yah hahm buh, _____ Oh, see yah hahm buh

56. WE ARE SINGING

for the Lord is our light. — We are sing-ing, _____
koo kah nigh nee kwen kohs. — *See yah hahm buh,* _____

Oh, we are sing-ing, for the Lord is our light. —
Oh, see yah hahm buh koo kah nigh nee kwen kohs. —

Verses

1. The Lord is the strength of our lives; ___
2. One thing have we asked of the Lord, ___
3. When bur - dens are heav - y to bear, ___
4. We walk in the strength of the Lord, ___

of whom shall we be a - fraid? ___ Though
yes, this is the thing we seek: ___ To
our shel - ter is God a - lone. ___ Our
God's love ____ is ev - er sure. ___ We

foes may be near to de - stroy; ___ the
dwell in the house of the Lord; ___ to
feet are ____ lift - ed high; ___ yes,
shout that the world may hear, ___ we

Lord will be our light. _____
live with God for - ev - er. _____
high up - on a rock. _____
sing a joy - ful song. _____

56. WE ARE SINGING

We Bow Down

Songs of Praise

Words and Music by
Twila Paris

You are Lord of cre-a- tion and

Lord of my life, Lord of the land __ and the sea.

You were Lord of the heav - ens be - fore there was

time, And Lord of all lords you will be! We bow

down ____ and we wor - ship you, Lord. We bow

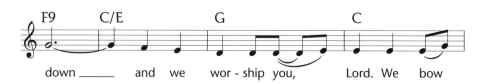

down ____ and we wor - ship you, Lord. We bow

57. WE BOW DOWN

down _____ and we wor - ship you, Lord,

Lord of all lords you will be!

You are

57. **WE BOW DOWN**

I Bow Down

Songs of Praise

Words and Music by
Walt Harrah

We Bring the Sacrifice of Praise

Ps. 116:17; Heb. 13:15
Songs of Praise

Words and Music by
Kirk Dearman

We bring the sac - ri - fice of praise in - to the

house of the Lord; We bring the sac - ri - fice of

praise in - to the house of the Lord. And we

of - fer up to you the sac - ri - fic - es of

thanks - giv - ing; And we of - fer up to you

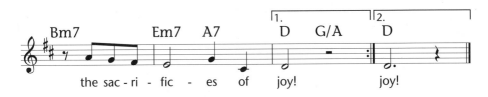

the sac - ri - fic - es of joy! joy!

59. WE BRING THE SACRIFICE OF PRAISE

With My Whole Heart

Zeph. 3:14
Songs of Praise

Words and Music by
Danny Chambers

With my whole heart, I will re-joice, with a

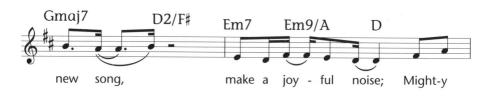

new song, make a joy-ful noise; Might-y

Sav-ior, I will bless your name, you have

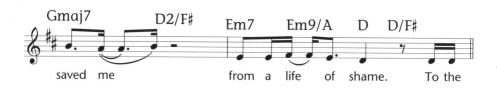

saved me from a life of shame. To the

God of my sal-va-tion I make this dec-la-ra-tion,

"You a-lone are the Lord of all.

60. WITH MY WHOLE HEART

You a - lone are the Lord of all.

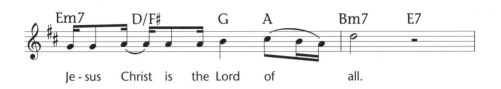

Je - sus Christ is the Lord of all.

Je - sus Christ is the Lord of all.

Je-sus Christ is the Lord of all."

60. WITH MY WHOLE HEART

Change My Heart, O God

Isa. 64:8
Confession

Words and music by
Eddie Espinosa

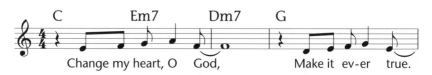

Change my heart, O God, Make it ev-er true.

Change my heart, O God, May I be like you.

You are the pot - ter, I am the clay, —

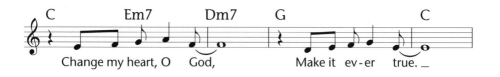

Mold me and make me, This is what I pray.

Change my heart, O God, Make it ev-er true. —

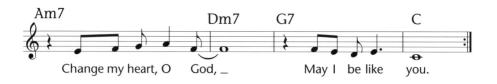

Change my heart, O God, — May I be like you.

61. CHANGE MY HEART, O GOD

Kyrie Eleison

Confession

Words: Ancient Greek liturgy
Music: Russian Orthodox liturgy

Ky - ri - e   e - lei - son.   Ky - ri - e   e -

lei - son.   Ky - ri - e   e - le - i - son.

Lord, Have Mercy

Confession

Words and music by
Jim Strathdee

Lord,   have   mer - cy.   Christ,   have   mer - cy.

Lord,   have   mer - cy   up - on   us.

Come to Me

Matt. 11:28–30
Confession

Music by
Walt Harrah

64. **COME TO ME**

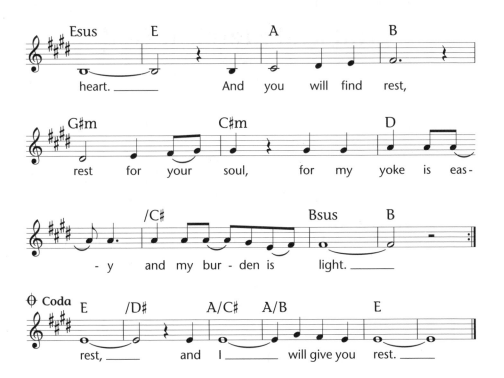

heart. _____ And you will find rest,

rest for your soul, for my yoke is eas-

- y and my bur-den is light. _____

Coda

rest, _____ and I _____ will give you rest. _____

64. COME TO ME

Kind and Merciful God

Confession

Words by Bryan Jeffrey Leech, 1973
Music: Traditional Swedish melody;
adapt. Bryan Jeffrey Leech, 1973

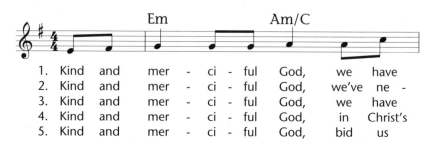

1. Kind	and	mer	-	ci - ful	God,	we	have
2. Kind	and	mer	-	ci - ful	God,	we've	ne -
3. Kind	and	mer	-	ci - ful	God,	we	have
4. Kind	and	mer	-	ci - ful	God,	in	Christ's
5. Kind	and	mer	-	ci - ful	God,	bid	us

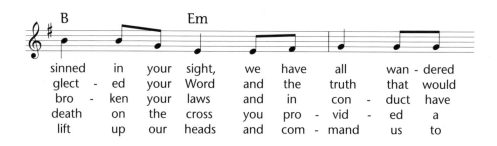

sinned	in	your	sight,	we	have	all	wan - dered
glect -	ed	your	Word	and	the	truth	that would
bro -	ken	your	laws	and	in	con -	duct have
death	on	the	cross	you	pro -	vid -	ed a
lift	up	our	heads	and	com -	mand	us to

far	from	your	way;	we	have	fol -	lowed de -
guide	us	a -	right;	we	have	lived	in the
veered	from	the	norm;	we	have	dreamed	of the
cleans -	ing	from	sin;	speak	the	words	that for -
rise	from	our	knees;	may	our	hearts	now be

65. KIND AND MERCIFUL GOD

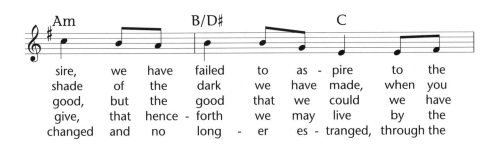

sire,	we	have	failed	to	as -	pire	to	the
shade	of	the	dark	we	have	made,	when	you
good,	but	the	good	that	we	could	we	have
give,	that	hence -	forth	we	may	live	by	the
changed	and	no	long -	er	es -	tranged,	through the

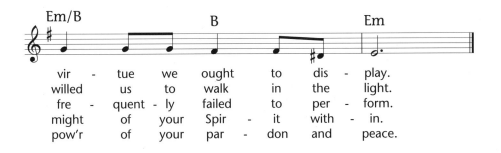

vir -	tue	we	ought	to	dis -	play.
willed	us	to	walk	in	the	light.
fre -	quent - ly	failed	to	per -	form.
might	of	your	Spir -	it	with -	in.
pow'r	of	your	par -	don	and	peace.

65. **KIND AND MERCIFUL GOD**

Refiner's Fire

1 John 3:1–7
Confession

Words and Music by
Brian Doerksen

There's a Place

Confession

Words and Music by
Kevin Boyd

1. There's a place of hon - es - ty and peace;
2. There's an ad - vo - cate, a throne of grace;
3. There's a place where wound - ed souls can mend,

Je - sus calls us. A place where bur - dens
Je - sus calls us. A source of strength, a
Je - sus calls us. A place of mer - cy

find re - lease; The Spir - it draws us.
warm em - brace; The Spir - it draws us.
with - out end; The Spir - it draws us.

Heal - ing flood of for - give - ness, Wash a -
Rush - ing wind of God's fa - vor, fill our

way our ev - 'ry stain; Through the blood of our
wan - d'ring hearts with faith; Through the blood of our

Sav - ior, Make us whole a - gain.
Sav - ior, Make us whole a - gain.

67. THERE'S A PLACE

Healing Grace

Confession/Forgiveness

Words and music by
Gary Sadler and John Chisum

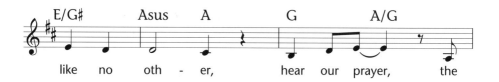

D   G/D   D   A/D   D   Bm

Mer - ci - ful God and Fa - ther, lov - ing us

E/G♯   Asus   A   G   A/G

like no oth - er, hear our prayer, the

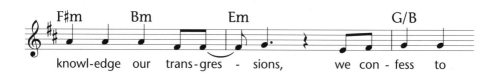

F♯m   Bm   Em   G   Asus   A

cry of our hearts, as we come to you. We ac -

F♯m   Bm   Em   G/B

knowl-edge our trans-gres - sions, we con - fess to

A/C♯   D   Bm   A

you our sins; ___ show us mer - cy and com-pas-

G2   D/F♯   G   Em   A   D

- sion, touch our lives with your heal-ing grace a - gain.

Re - lease us from the past ___ as we

seek your face: wash us clean at last. ___

We re - ceive your love, we re - ceive your heal - ing

grace. We re - ceive your love, we re -

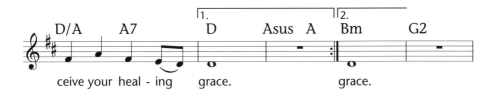

ceive your heal - ing grace. grace.

Touch our lives with your heal - ing grace a - gain.

68. HEALING GRACE

God Has Smiled on Me

Gal. 5:1, 13–25
Response to Forgiveness

Words and Music by
Isaiah Jones, Jr.

God has smiled on me.

He has set ____ me free, ____

God has smiled on me. He's been good

to me. ____ 1. 2.

69. GOD HAS SMILED ON ME

Abundant Life

John 10:10
Response to Forgiveness

Words and Music by
Josh A. Hailey and Isaiah Jones, Jr.
Arr. by Isaiah Jones, Jr.

A - bun - dant life, a - bun - dant life, a - bun - dant life is

1. yours. Je - sus came to tell us
2. yours.

1. You must live ful - filled in Christ
2. Doubt keeps fear in your soul;

or you have no vic - t'ry in your life.
fear keeps you from know - ing you're whole.

Je - sus Christ o - pens all doors, a -

bun - dant life is yours. The word of God will tell you

70. ABUNDANT LIFE

Bless the Lord, My Soul

Ps. 103
Response to Forgiveness

Words and Music by
The Taizé Community

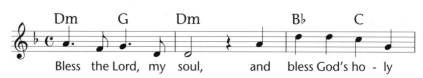

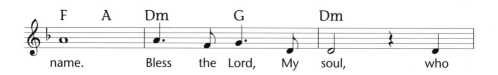

Bless the Lord, my soul, and bless God's ho - ly

name. Bless the Lord, My soul, who

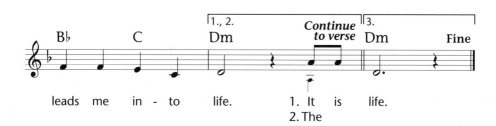

leads me in - to life.   1. It is life.
                         2. The

(1.) he who for-gives all your guilt, who heals ev - 'ry

one of your ills, who re - deems your life from the

grave, who crowns you with love and com - pas - sion.

71.   BLESS THE LORD, MY SOUL

(2.) Lord is com-pas-sion and love, slow to an-ger and rich in

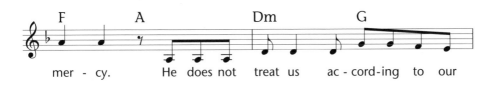

mer - cy. He does not treat us ac - cord-ing to our

sins nor re - pay us ac-cord-ing to our faults.

Glory to God

Ps. 105:1–4
Response to Forgiveness

Words and Music by
Jim Strathdee

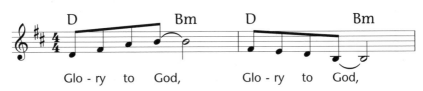

Glo - ry to God, Glo - ry to God,

praise and al - le - lu - ia. Glo - ry to God,

Glo - ry to God, praise the name of the Lord. _

72. GLORY TO GOD

Glory, Praises!

Response to Forgiveness

Words and Music by
Kevin Boyd

73. GLORY, PRAISES!

Glory, Glory, Hallelujah!

Matt. 11:28
Response to Forgiveness

Words and Music traditional

1. Glo - ry, glo - ry, _____ hal - le - lu - jah!
2. I feel bet - ter, _____ so much bet - ter
3. Feel like shout - ing, _____ "Hal - le - lu - jah!"

Since I laid my _____ bur - den down.
Since I laid my _____ bur - den down.
Since I laid my _____ bur - den down.

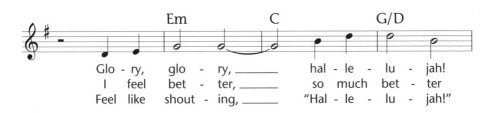

Glo - ry, glo - ry, _____ hal - le - lu - jah!
I feel bet - ter, _____ so much bet - ter
Feel like shout - ing, _____ "Hal - le - lu - jah!"

Since I laid my bur - den down.
Since I laid my bur - den down.
Since I laid my bur - den down.

I Will Sing of the Mercies

Ps. 89:1, 5, 8
Response to Forgiveness

Music by
James H. Fillmore

I will sing of the mer-cies of the Lord for - ev - er, I will

sing, I will sing. I will sing of the mer-cies of the

Lord for - ev - er, I will sing of the mer-cies of the

Lord. With my mouth I will make known

your faith - ful-ness, your faith - ful-ness; With my

mouth I will make known your faith-ful-ness to

75. I WILL SING OF THE MERCIES

all gen-er - a - tions. I will sing of the mer-cies of the

Lord for - ev - er, I will sing of the mer-cies of the Lord.

Grace Greater Than Our Sin

Rom. 5:20
Response to Forgiveness

Words by Julia H. Johnston
Music by Daniel B. Towner

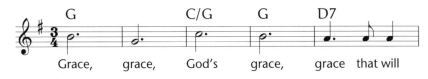

Grace, grace, God's grace, grace that will

par - don and cleanse with - in; Grace, grace, God's

grace, grace that is great - er than all our sin.

Justified Freely

Rom. 5:8–10
Response to Forgiveness/Justification

Music by
Walt Harrah

All have sinned, fall - en short

of the glo - ry of God, __ of the

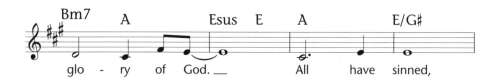

glo - ry of God. __ All have sinned,

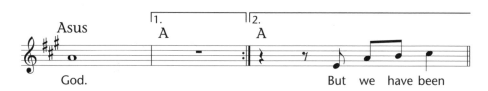

fall - en short of the glo - ry of

God. But we have been

jus - ti - fied free - ly by his grace, by the

77. JUSTIFIED FREELY

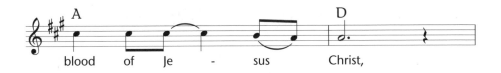

blood of Je - sus Christ,

jus - ti - fied free - ly by his grace.

But we have been grace.

There Is a Redeemer

Phil. 2:9
Response to Forgiveness

Words and Music by
Melody Green

78.   THERE IS A REDEEMER

glo - ry, I will see his face,

There I'll serve my King for-ev-er in that ho-ly

place. Thank you, oh, my Fa - ther, for

giv-ing us your Son, and leav - ing your

Spir - it 'til the work on earth is done and

leav - ing your Spir - it 'til the work on earth is done.

78. THERE IS A REDEEMER

Once for All

Rom. 5:1–11
Response to Forgiveness

Words and Music by
Walt Harrah

E ... F#m

We have been made ho - ly,

B ... E ... C#m

spot-less, un - de - filed ... by the blood of

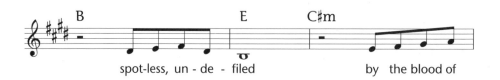

F#m ... B ... A ... E

Je - sus ... once for all. ___ ... We have been for-

F#m ... B ... E ... C#m

giv - en, ... we've been re - con - ciled

F#m ... B ... A ... E ... Fine

by the blood of Je - sus ... once for all. ___

D/E ... E ... A ... Am

Once for all ... there at Cal - va - ry

79. ONCE FOR ALL

Je - sus died for hu - man - i - ty,

bear - ing there all our guilt and our dis - grace.

Once for all by the sav - ing blood

we've been washed in its cleans - ing flood.

Bold - ly now we ap - proach the throne of grace.

79. ONCE FOR ALL

Oh Lord, You're Beautiful

Response to Forgiveness

Words and Music by
Keith Green

Oh Lord, you're beau - ti - ful, _____

___ your face is all I seek. _____

For when your eyes are on this

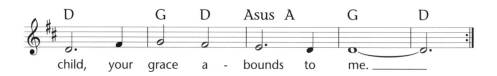

child, your grace a - bounds to me. _____

80. OH LORD, YOU'RE BEAUTIFUL

Surely It Is God

Isa. 12:2
Response to Forgiveness

Music by
Jack Noble White
Adapted from "The First Song of Isaiah"

Sure - ly it is God who saves me; I will

trust in him and not be a - fraid, For the

Lord is my strong-hold and my sure de - fense, and

he will be my Sav - ior.

81. SURELY IT IS GOD

Be Still and Know

Ex. 15:26; Ps. 46:10
The Word/Call to Worship/Prayer

Words: St. 1, 2 Anon.; st. 3, 4, 5 by Sylvia Washer
Music: Arr. by Lee Herrington and Tom Fettke

1. Be still and know that I am
2. I am the Lord that heal - eth
3. I nev - er shall for - sake my
4. I'll keep you in my per - fect

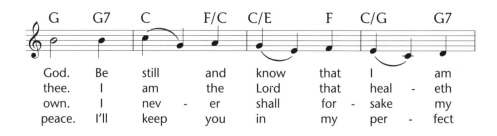

God. Be still and know that I am
thee. I am the Lord that heal - eth
own. I nev - er shall for - sake my
peace. I'll keep you in my per - fect

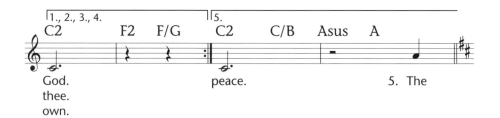

God. Be still and know that I am
thee. I am the Lord that heal - eth
own. I nev - er shall for - sake my
peace. I'll keep you in my per - fect

1., 2., 3., 4. | 5.

God.   peace.   5. The
thee.
own.

82. BE STILL AND KNOW

joy   I   give   shall   be   your   strength. The

joy   I   give   shall   be   your   strength. The

joy   I   give   shall   be   your   strength.

82. BE STILL AND KNOW

Our God Is Mighty

Ex. 15:1–9; Matt. 28:19; Acts 2:14
The Word/Affirmation of Faith

Words and Music by
Jim Gill

83. OUR GOD IS MIGHTY

2. Jer - i - cho's walls ___ came tum-bling down
4. When they were to - geth - er in one ac - cord

When the peo-ple's prais - es be-gan to re - sound. ___
The ___ Ho - ly - Spir - it on them ___ was poured.

___ Strong-holds are fall - ing the world a - round ___
___ To give them pow - er to share their Lord. ___

'Cause our God is a might - y God.
Our God is a might - y God.

3. Je - sus walked on wa - ter and calmed the
5. Go ___ make dis - ci - ples of ev - 'ry

sea. ___ He broke the walls down
na - tion. Bap - tize and give them

be - tween you and me. ___ He brought us to -
a sure ___ foun - da - tion. ___ Bring ___ them to -

geth - er so our world could see ___ That
geth - er for ___ great cel - e - bra - tions, ___ 'Cause

To Refrain

our God is a might - y God. Our God is
our God is a might - y God.

83. OUR GOD IS MIGHTY

Our God Reigns

Isa. 52:7, 53; Luke 24: 5, 6, 39
The Word

Words and Music by
Lenny Smith
Arr. by Stephen A. Beddia

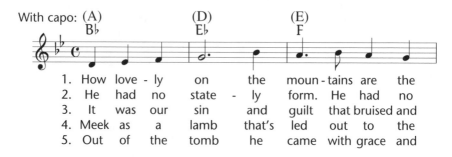

1. How love-ly on the moun-tains are the
2. He had no state-ly form. He had no
3. It was our sin and guilt that bruised and
4. Meek as a lamb that's led out to the
5. Out of the tomb he came with grace and

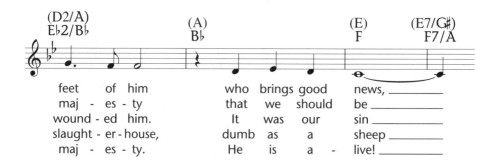

feet of him who brings good news, _____
maj - es - ty that we should be _____
wound-ed him. It was our sin _____
slaught-er-house, dumb as a sheep _____
maj - es - ty. He is a - live! _____

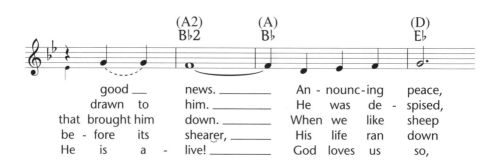

good __ news. _____ An - nounc-ing peace,
drawn to him. _____ He was de - spised,
that brought him down. _____ When we like sheep
be - fore its shearer, _____ His life ran down
He is a - live! _____ God loves us so,

84. OUR GOD REIGNS

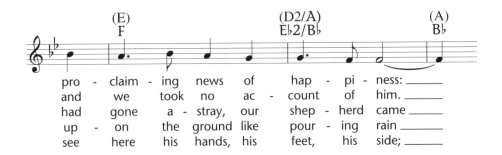

pro - claim - ing news of hap - pi - ness: _____
and we took no ac - count of him. _____
had gone a - stray, our shep - herd came _____
up - on the ground like pour - ing rain _____
see here his hands, his feet, his side; _____

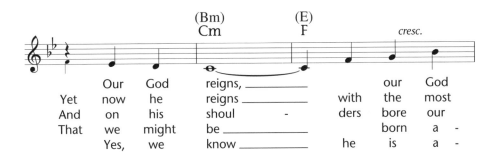

    Our God reigns, _____ our God
Yet now he reigns _____ with the most
And on his shoul - ders bore our
That we might be _____ born a -
Yes, we know _____ he is a -

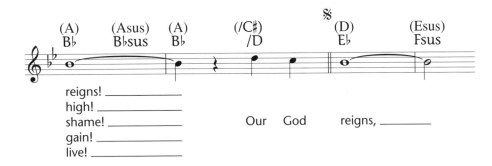

reigns! _____
high! _____
shame! _____ Our God reigns, _____
gain! _____
live! _____

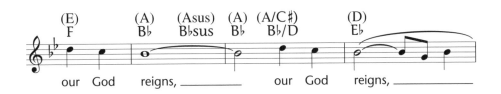

our God reigns, _____ our God reigns, _____

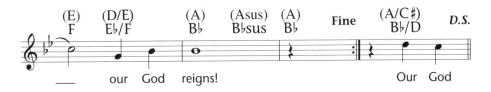

_____ our God reigns! Our God

84. OUR GOD REIGNS

Thy Word

Ps. 119:105
The Word/Prayer/Affirmation of Faith

Words by Amy Grant
Music by Michael W. Smith

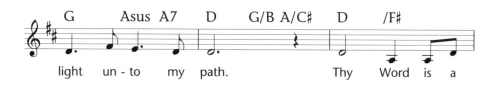

Thy Word is a lamp un-to my feet and a

light un-to my path. Thy Word is a

lamp un-to my feet and a light un-to my path.

When I feel a-fraid, think I've lost my way,

Still you're there right be-side _____ me. And

nothing will I fear as long as you are near,

85. THY WORD

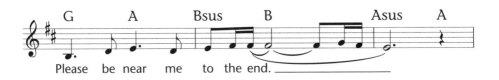
Please be near me to the end. _____

Thy Word is a lamp un - to my feet and a

light un - to my path.

Thy Word is a lamp un - to my feet and a

light un - to my path. Thy Word is a

lamp un - to my feet and a light un - to my path.

She Flies On!

Gen. 1:2; Joel 2:8–29; Luke 1:35–38; Acts 2:2–8
The Word/Pentecost/Advent/Christmas

Words and Music by
Gordon Light
Arr. by Darryl Nixon

She comes sail-ing on the wind, her wings

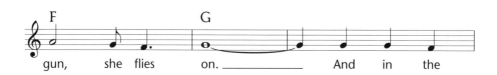

flash-ing in the sun; on a jour-ney just be-

gun, she flies on. _____ And in the

pas-sage of her flight, her song rings out through the

night, full of laugh-ter, full of light, she flies on.

1.   Si - lent wa-ters rock-ing _____ on the
2.   Man - y were the dream-ers _____ whose
3. To a gen - tle girl in Gal - i - lee a _____

86. SHE FLIES ON!

morn - ing of our birth, like an emp - ty cra - dle
eyes were giv - en sight, when the Spir - it filled their
gen - tle breeze she came, ___ a whis - per soft - ly

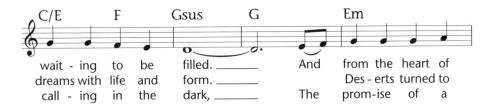

wait - ing to be filled. ___ And from the heart of
dreams with life and form. ___ Des - erts turned to
call - ing in the dark, ___ The prom - ise of a

God the Spir - it moved up - on the earth, like a
gar - dens, brok - en hearts found new de - light, and then
child of peace whose reign would nev - er end, Mar - y

moth - er breath-ing life in - to her child. ___
down the a - ges still ___ she flew on. ___
sang the Spir - it song with - in her heart. ___

86. SHE FLIES ON!

On Eagles' Wings

Ex. 19:4; Ps. 17:8; 91:1–6, 14–16
The Word/Psalm/Affirmation of Faith/Funeral

Words and music by
Michael Joncas

And he will raise you up on ea - gles' wings,

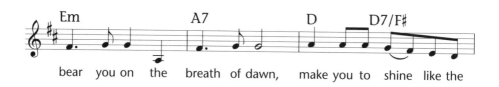

bear you on the breath of dawn, make you to shine like the

sun, and hold you in the palm of his hand.

Last time continue

And hold you, hold you in the

palm _____ of his hand. _____

87. ON EAGLES' WINGS

In the Bulb There Is a Flower

John 11:17–44; 1 Cor. 15:51–54a; 2 Cor. 5:16–21
Response to the Word

Words and Music by
Natalie Sleeth

88. IN THE BULB THERE IS A FLOWER

Here I Stand

Luke 11:9; Rev. 3:20
Response to the Word/Communion

Words and Music by
The Iona Community

Em — Am — D — Em — C

Here I stand at the door _____ and knock, _____
Here I stand at the door and

F#m — B — Em — Am — D

___ and knock. I will come and dine _____
knock, and knock. I will dine with

Em — Am7 — B — Em

___ with those who ask me in.
those who ask me in.

I Believe in Jesus

Response to the Word

Words and Music by
Marc Nelson

E — A — Bsus — B — E

I be-lieve in Je - sus, I be-lieve he
(you, Lord,) (you

Let Me Have My Way among You

Col. 3:15; Heb. 4:6–11
Response to the Word

Words and Music by
Graham Kendrick

Lay It All Down

Phil. 3:7–10
Response to the Word/Ordination

Words and Music by
Brian Marsh

Resting in You

Ps. 63:1–8
Response to the Word/Funeral/Affirmation of Faith

Words and Music by
Ed Beaty and Lenny Smith

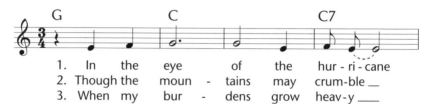

1. In the eye of the hur - ri - cane
2. Though the moun - tains may crum-ble __
3. When my bur - dens grow heav-y ___

I find peace in __ the storm. I
and the sea roll __ a - way,
and I bend be-neath the load,

Trust - ing in you, Lord, my __ soul
know you are with me, through the night
your strength will help me down the long,

is re - born. Like a child ___ in your
and the day. For you're right ___ here in -
dust - y road. All my trials and trib - u -

arms, __ safe and warm a - gainst the night.
side me; yes, you live with - in my heart.
la - tions, they can on - ly make me strong.

93. RESTING IN YOU

You will bear me through the dark -
I've a - ban - doned my life in -
For you lift my soul with glad -

ness, sur - ound - ed by your light.
to your gen - tle, lov - ing arms.
ness, and fill my heart with song.

Rest - ing in you, Lord, safe

in your arms. Rest - ing in

you, Lord, I am safe in your arms.

93. RESTING IN YOU

Love Is a Circle

Response to the Word

Words and Music by
Peggy Brown

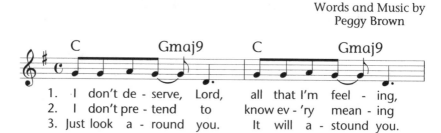

1. I don't de - serve, Lord, all that I'm feel - ing,
2. I don't pre - tend to know ev - 'ry mean - ing
3. Just look a - round you. It will a - stound you.

But, Lord, I know you're real. ____ You've
of ev - 'ry - thing God does. ____
See what God's love can do. ____

giv - en me hope, you've giv - en me heal - ing,
All I can do is trust that I'm lean - ing
Let that love fill you. Now let it com - pel you to

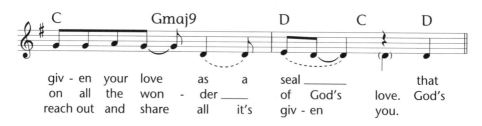

giv - en your love as a seal _____ that
on all the won - der ____ of God's love. God's
reach out and share all it's giv - en you.

Refrain

Love is a cir - cle, the heart of all that is

real.   Love   is   a   cir - cle,   and

what   you   give you will   feel. ___

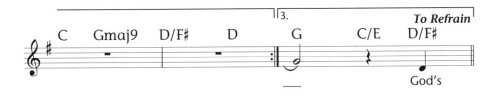

___   God's

___   And   what   you   give you will   feel. ___

Sovereign Lord

Ps. 71:5–6
Response to the Word

Words and Music by
Dave Hopkins

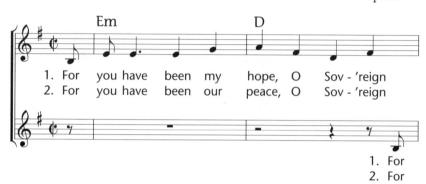

1. For you have been my hope, O Sov - 'reign
2. For you have been our peace, O Sov - 'reign

1. For
2. For

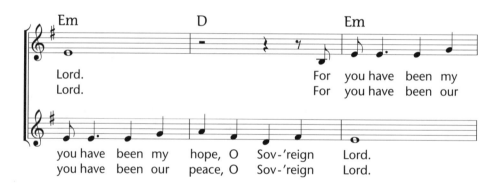

Lord.
Lord.

For you have been my
For you have been our

you have been my hope, O Sov-'reign Lord.
you have been our peace, O Sov-'reign Lord.

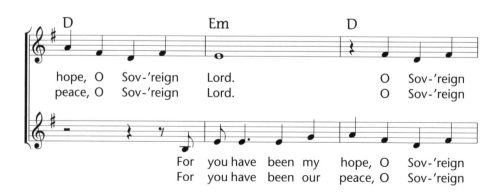

hope, O Sov-'reign Lord.   O Sov-'reign
peace, O Sov-'reign Lord.   O Sov-'reign

For you have been my hope, O Sov-'reign
For you have been our peace, O Sov-'reign

95. SOVEREIGN LORD

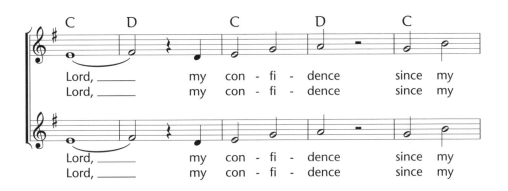

Lord, _____ my con - fi - dence since my
Lord, _____ my con - fi - dence since my

Lord, _____ my con - fi - dence since my
Lord, _____ my con - fi - dence since my

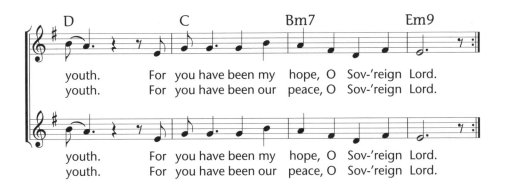

youth. For you have been my hope, O Sov-'reign Lord.
youth. For you have been our peace, O Sov-'reign Lord.

youth. For you have been my hope, O Sov-'reign Lord.
youth. For you have been our peace, O Sov-'reign Lord.

95. SOVEREIGN LORD

Love the Lord Your God

Deut. 6:5; Matt. 22:37, 38
Response to the Word

Words and Music by
Jean and Jim Strathdee

Love the Lord your God _____ with

all your heart. _____ Love the Lord your

God _____ with all your soul. _____

Love the Lord your God _____ with all

your mind. _____ Love the Lord your

G#m7 C#m7 A B E

God _____ with all that you are. _____

What Does the Lord Require?

Micah 6:8
Response to the Word/Departing/Ordination

Words and Music by
Jim Strathdee
Adapted by
Linda White

① Bb / F / Gm

What does the Lord re - quire of

Dm / Eb / Bb / Cm / F

you? What does the Lord re - quire of

② Bb / Bb / F/A / Gm / Dm/F

you? To seek jus - tice and love kind-ness

③

Jus - tice, kind - ness,

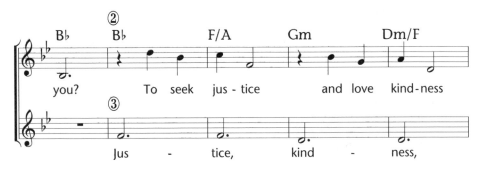

Eb / Bb/D / Cm7 / F / Bb

and walk hum - bly with your God.

walk hum - bly with your God.

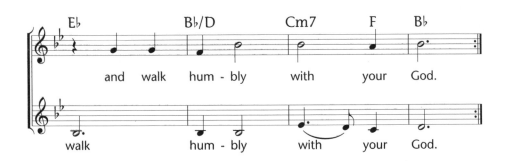

97. WHAT DOES THE LORD REQUIRE?

The River Is Here

John 4:13–14; 7:37–38; Rev. 22:1–3
Response to the Word

Words and Music by
Andy Park

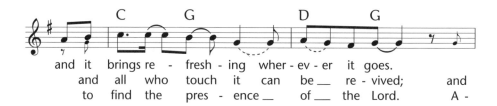

1. Down the moun-tain the riv - er __ flows
2. The riv - er of God __ is teem-ing with life
3. Up to the moun-tain we love to __ go

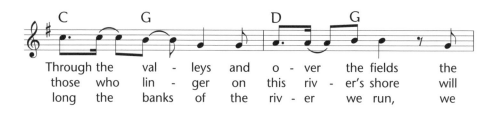

and it brings re - fresh - ing wher-ev-er it goes.
and all who touch it can be __ re - vived; and
to find the pres - ence __ of __ the Lord. A -

Through the val - leys and o - ver the fields the
those who lin - ger on this riv - er's shore will
long the banks of the riv - er we run, we

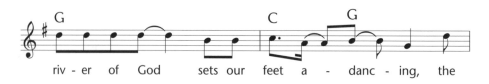

riv - er is rush-ing and the riv - er is here. The
come back thirst - ing for more of the Lord. The
dance with laugh - ter giv-ing praise to the Son. The

riv - er of God sets our feet a - danc - ing, the

riv - er of God   fills our hears with   cheer.   The

riv - er of God   fills our mouths with   laugh - ter,   and

3rd time continue

we   re - joice   for the riv - er is here.

and   we   re - joice   for the   riv - er is   here.

98. THE RIVER IS HERE

Center of My Life

Psalm 16
Prayer

Words and Music by
Paul Inwood

Em   D/F#   G   B

O Lord, you are the cen-ter of my life:

D   A   Bm   F#m

I will al-ways praise you, I will al-ways serve you,

G   Em   B

I will al-ways keep you in my sight.

99. CENTER OF MY LIFE

Dona Nobis Pacem

Prayer

Music: Unknown

*Pronounced "pachem." The Latin phrase means "Grant us peace."

In His Presence

Prayer

Words and Music by
Dick and Melodie Tunney

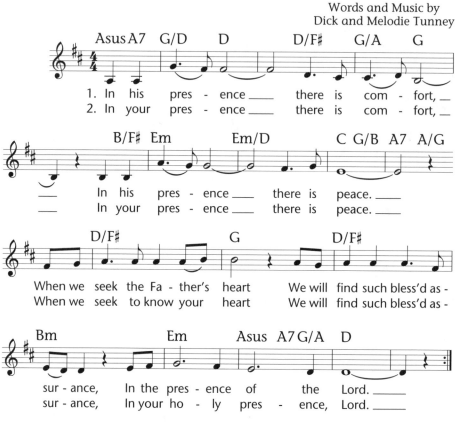

1. In his pres - ence ____ there is com - fort, __
2. In your pres - ence ____ there is com - fort, __

____ In his pres - ence ____ there is peace. ____
____ In your pres - ence ____ there is peace. ____

When we seek the Fa - ther's heart   We will find such bless'd as -
When we seek to know your heart   We will find such bless'd as -

sur - ance, In the pres - ence of the Lord. ____
sur - ance, In your ho - ly pres - ence, Lord. ____

Gentle Shepherd, Come and Lead Us

John 10:1–30
Prayer

Words and Music by
Gloria and William Gaither

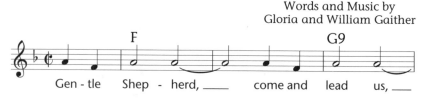

Gen - tle Shep - herd, ____ come and lead us, ____

102. GENTLE SHEPHERD, COME AND LEAD US

God, In Your Loving Mercy

Prayer

Words and Music by
Jim Strathdee

God, in your lov - ing mer - cy, hear our prayer.

Healer of My Soul

Isa. 57:18; Matt. 13:1–9, 18–23
Prayer

Words and Music by
John Talbot

1. Heal - er of my soul, _____
2. Keep - er of my soul, _____

Keep me at ev - en', ____ Keep me at
On rough course far - ing. ____ Help __ and

morn - ing, ____ Keep me at noon, Heal - er
safe - guard my means __ this night, Keep - er

104. **HEALER OF MY SOUL**

God of Mercy

Prayer

Words and Music by
Bob Hurd

Hear our prayer. Hear our prayer.

Hear our prayer. Hear us, O

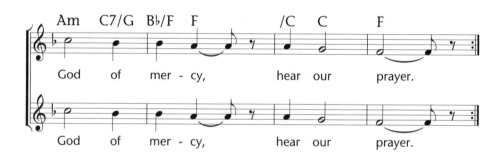

God of mer - cy, hear our prayer.

God of mer - cy, hear our prayer.

105. GOD OF MERCY

Hear Us, O God (Oyenos, Mi Dios)

Prayer

Words by Owen Alstott, Spanish trans. by Mary F. Reza
Music by Bob Hurd and Owen Alstott

1. Hear us, O God, Hear us, O God.
2. O - ye - nos, mi Dios, O - ye - nos, mi Dios.

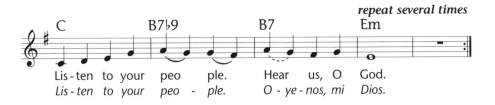

repeat several times

Lis - ten to your peo ple. Hear us, O God.
Lis - ten to your peo - ple. O - ye - nos, mi Dios.

106. HEAR US, O GOD (OYENOS, MI DIOS)

In the Secret

Phil. 3:10–14
Prayer

Words and Music by
Andy Park

107.   IN THE SECRET

Spirit, Now Live in Me

Matt. 3:16
Liturgical Year/Pentecost

Words and Music by
Bryan Jeffery Leech, 1976

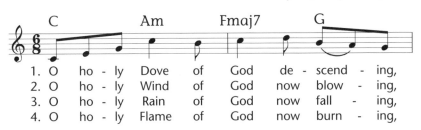

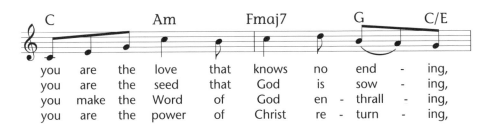

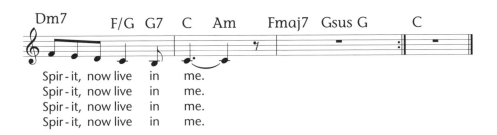

1. O ho-ly Dove of God de-scend-ing,
2. O ho-ly Wind of God now blow-ing,
3. O ho-ly Rain of God now fall-ing,
4. O ho-ly Flame of God now burn-ing,

you are the love that knows no end-ing,
you are the seed that God is sow-ing,
you make the Word of God en-thrall-ing,
you are the power of Christ re-turn-ing,

all of our shat-tered dreams you're mend-ing:
you are the life that starts us grow-ing:
you are that in-ner voice now call-ing:
you are the an-swer to our yearn-ing:

Spir-it, now live in me.
Spir-it, now live in me.
Spir-it, now live in me.
Spir-it, now live in me.

Make Me a Channel of Your Peace

John 14:23–28; Rom. 14:13–19
Prayer

Prayer of St. Francis
Music by Sebastian Temple

109. MAKE ME A CHANNEL OF YOUR PEACE

To be under-stood as to under-stand, ___

___ To be loved as to love with all my soul. ___

3. Make me a chan-nel of your peace. ___ It is in par-don-

ing that we are par-doned, ___ In giv-ing to

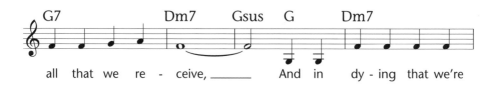
all that we re-ceive, ___ And in dy-ing that we're

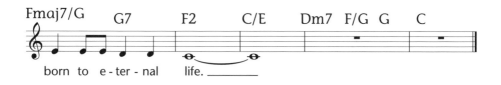
born to e-ter-nal life. ___

109. MAKE ME A CHANNEL OF YOUR PEACE

Lord, Listen to Your Children Praying

Ps. 17:6
Prayer

Words and Music by
Ken Medema

Lord, lis-ten to your child-ren pray - ing,

Lord, send your Spir - it in this place;

Lord, lis-ten to your child-ren pray - ing, send us

love, send us pow'r, send us grace. grace,

send us love, send us pow'r, send us grace.

110. LORD, LISTEN TO YOUR CHILDREN PRAYING

O Lord, Hear My Prayer

Ps. 102:1, 2
Prayer

Words and Music by
The Taizé Community

O Lord, hear my prayer, O Lord, hear my prayer.

When I call, an - swer me. O Lord, hear my prayer, O

Lord, hear my prayer. Come and lis - ten to me.

The Lord is my song, the Lord is my praise:

All my hope comes from God. The Lord is my song, the

Lord is my praise: God, the well-spring of life.

111. O LORD, HEAR MY PRAYER

Remember Me

Luke 23:42
Prayer/Holy Week

Words and Music: Traditional

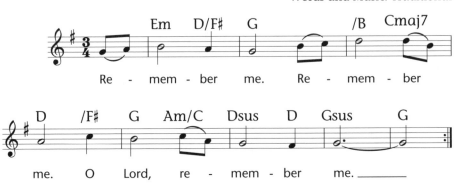

Re - mem - ber me. Re - mem - ber
me. O Lord, re - mem - ber me. _____

The Lord's Prayer

Matt. 6:9–13
Prayer

Music by
Christy Weir

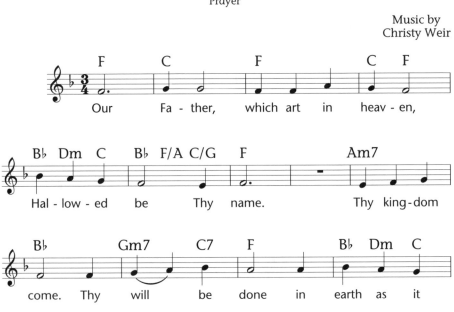

Our Fa - ther, which art in heav - en,
Hal - low - ed be Thy name. Thy king - dom
come. Thy will be done in earth as it

112. REMEMBER ME   **113. THE LORD'S PRAYER**

is in heav'n. Give us this day our daily bread, and for-give us our debts, as we for-give our debt-ors. And lead us not in-to temp-ta-tion, but de-liv-er us from e-vil; for thine is the king-dom, and the pow-er and the glo-ry, for-ev-er and ev-er, A-men. For-ev-er and ev-er, A-men.

113. THE LORD'S PRAYER

Give Thanks with a Grateful Heart

Ps. 126:3
Offering and Thanksgiving

Words and Music by
Henry Smith

Give thanks with a grate-ful heart, give

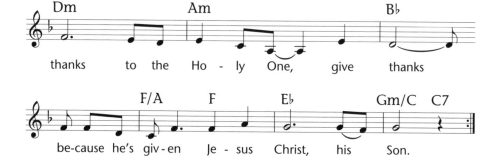

thanks to the Ho - ly One, give thanks

be-cause he's giv-en Je - sus Christ, his Son.

And now let the weak say, "I am strong;"

let the poor say, "I am rich" be - cause of

what the Lord has done for us.

Give thanks, give thanks, give thanks!

114.   GIVE THANKS WITH A GRATEFUL HEART

Everything Is Yours, Lord

1 Chron. 29:9–17; Ps. 138:1–8
Offering and Thanksgiving

Words: Zambian offertory
Arrangement: Geoff Weaver

Ev-'ry-thing is yours, Lord; ev-'ry-thing comes from you:
Ta - ta po - ke - le - la If - ya bu - pe fye - su:

all we have we of - fer _____ to you. Ac-cept our love, Lord,
If - yo twa - mi pe - la _____ le - lo. Po - ke - le - le - ni _____

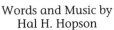

_____ we pray; re - ceive our gifts, Lord, _____ to - day.
_____ ta - ta, Po - ke - le - le - ni _____ le - lo.

Shout for Joy to God

Ps. 100:1–2
Offering and Thanksgiving

Words and Music by
Hal H. Hopson

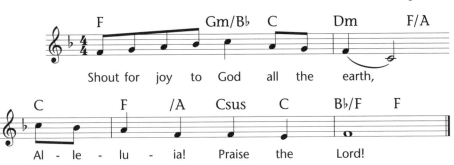

Shout for joy to God all the earth,

Al - le - lu - ia! Praise the Lord!

115. EVERYTHING IS YOURS, LORD 116. SHOUT FOR JOY TO GOD

Take Up Your Cross

Matt. 16:24–27; Mark 8:34–38; 10:21; Luke 9:23–25; Eph. 6:11–17
Offering and Thanksgiving

Words and Music by
Kinley Lange

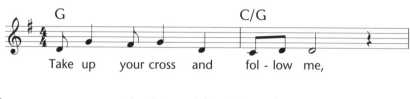

Take up your cross and fol - low me,

lift up the yoke of your sal - va - tion, put on the ar - mor

of the Word, and walk in the Truth and Light.

What would it prof - it you _____ to gain the world

___ for a day? If you would have your life,

___ first, you must give it a - way.

Take up your cross and fol-low me, lift up the yoke of

117. **TAKE UP YOUR CROSS**

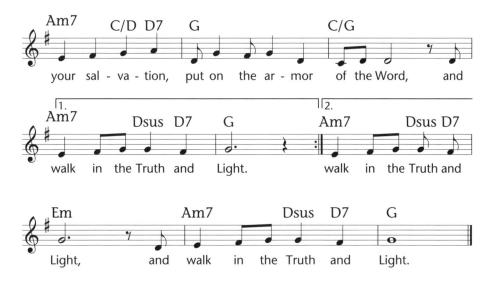

your sal - va - tion, put on the ar - mor of the Word, and

1. walk in the Truth and Light. 2. walk in the Truth and

Light, and walk in the Truth and Light.

We Are an Offering

Offering and Thanksgiving

Words and Music by
Dwight Liles

We lift our voi - ces, we lift our hands, we lift our

lives up to you, we are an of - fer - ing. Lord, use our

voi - ces, Lord, use our hands, Lord, use our

lives, they are yours, we are an of - fer - ing.

118. WE ARE AN OFFERING

All that we have, all that we are,

all that we hope to be, we give to you, we

give to you. We lift our voi - ces,

we lift our hands, we lift our lives up to you,

we are an of-fer-ing, we are an of-fer-ing.

118. WE ARE AN OFFERING

Lamb of God
(Good Shepherd Mass)

John 1:29
Communion/Agnus Dei

Music by Owen Alstott
Good Shepherd Mass

Lamb of God, you take a - way the

sins of the world: have mer - cy on us.

Lamb of God, you take a - way the

sins of the world: have mer - cy on us.

Lamb of God, you take a - way the

sins of the world: grant us peace.

119. LAMB OF GOD (GOOD SHEPHERD MASS)

Lamb of God

1 Peter 1:18–19
Communion/Agnus Dei

Words and Music by
Twila Paris

1. Your only Son, no sin to hide,
But you have sent him from your side, To walk up-
on this guilt-y sod, And to be called the Lamb of God.

2. Your gift of love, they cru-ci-fied,
They laughed and scorned him as he died. The hum-ble
King they named a fraud And sac-ri-ficed the Lamb of God.

3. I was so lost, I should have died,
But you have brought me to your side, To be led
by your staff and rod, And to be called a lamb of God.

Refrain

O Lamb of God, sweet Lamb of God, I love the
ho-ly Lamb of God! O wash me in his pre-cious
blood, My Je-sus Christ the Lamb of God.

120. LAMB OF GOD

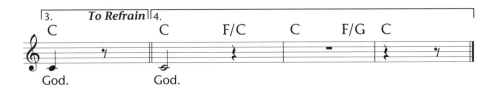

Agnus Dei

John 1:29, 36
Communion

Music by
The Iona Community

121. AGNUS DEI

Among Us and before Us

Matt. 26:26; 1 Cor. 11:23–26
Communion
Response to Pardon/Before Gospel/After Sermon/General Praise

Words and Music by
The Iona Community
Tune: *Gatehouse* (JLB)

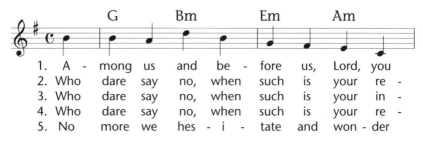

```
            G          Bm          Em          Am
1. A   -  mong  us    and   be - fore   us,   Lord,  you
2. Who    dare  say   no,   when  such   is   your   re -
3. Who    dare  say   no,   when  such   is   your   in -
4. Who    dare  say   no,   when  such   is   your   re -
5. No     more  we    hes - i - tate   and   won - der
```

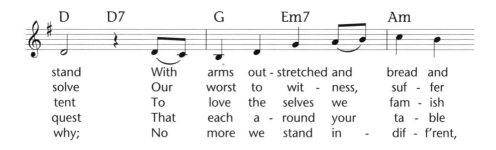

```
   D    D7              G         Em7            Am
stand          With   arms  out-stretched and  bread  and
solve          Our    worst  to   wit - ness,   suf - fer
tent           To     love   the  selves  we   fam - ish
quest          That   each   a - round  your    ta - ble
why;           No     more   we   stand  in -  dif - f'rent,
```

```
   /C        Am/D  D            G          Bm
wine   at   hand.    Con - front - ing  those  un -
and    ab - solve,   Our   best  to     raise  in
and    re - sent,    To    cra - dle    our    un -
should be   guest,   That  here  the    an - cient
scared or   shy.     Your  in - vi - ta - tion
```

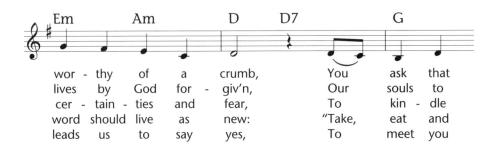

122. AMONG US AND BEFORE US

Bread, Blessed and Broken

1 Cor. 11:24
Communion

Words and Music by
Michael B. Lynch

123.   BREAD, BLESSED AND BROKEN

Great Thanksgiving (Land of Rest)

Communion/Great Thanksgiving

Music adapted by
Marcia Pruner, 1980

1. Ho - ly, ho - ly, ho - ly Lord,
2. Bless - ed is he who comes

God of pow-er and might, _____ heav-en and earth are
in the name of the Lord. Ho - san - na in the

full of your glo - ry. Ho - san - na in the high - est.
high - est, __ Ho - san - na in the high - est.

Leader: You are holy, O God of majesty, and blessed is your Son our Lord . . .
Great is the mystery of faith.

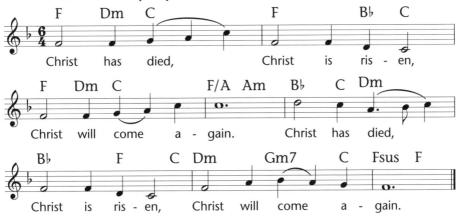

Christ has died, Christ is ris - en,

Christ will come a - gain. Christ has died,

Christ is ris - en, Christ will come a - gain.

Leader: Gracious God, pour out your Holy Spirit upon us . . .
Through Christ, with Christ, in Christ, in the unity of the Holy Spirit,
all glory and honor are yours, almighty Father, now and forever.

A - men, A - men, A - men.

124. GREAT THANKSGIVING (LAND OF REST)

Great Thanksgiving

Communion/Great Thanksgiving

Words and Music by
Leon Roberts

125. GREAT THANKSGIVING (Roberts)

Leader: You are holy, O God of majesty, and blessed is your Son our Lord . . .
Great is the mystery of faith.

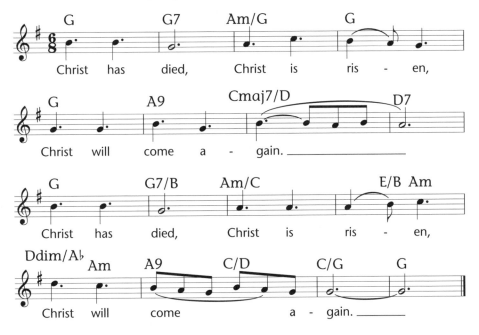

Leader: Gracious God, pour out your Holy Spirit upon us . . .
Through Christ, with Christ, in Christ, in the unity of the Holy Spirit,
all glory and honor are yours, almighty Father, now and forever.

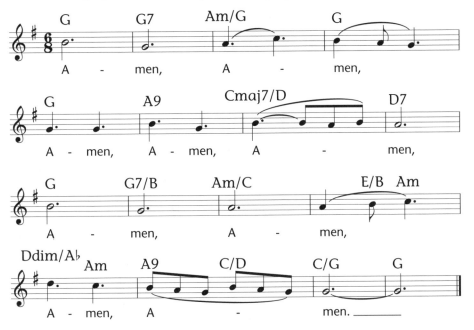

125. GREAT THANKSGIVING (Roberts)

Come, Share the Lord

Luke 22:17
Communion

Words and Music by
Jeffery Leech

Bb/C   F   Gm7

1. We gath-er here in Je-sus' name,
2. He joins us here, he breaks the bread,
3. We'll gath-er soon where an-gels sing;

F   F/A   Csus

his love is burn-ing in our hearts like liv-ing flame;
the Lord who pours the cup is ris-en from the dead;
we'll see the glo-ry of our Lord and com-ing King;

C7   F   C   F

for through his lov-ing Son the Fa-ther makes us one:
the one we love the most is now our grac-ious host:
now we an-tic-i-pate the feast for which we wait:

Bb   F/A   Gm   C   F   Fine

Come, take the bread, come, drink the wine, come, share the Lord.

C7   F   Bb/D Am/C C7/Bb F/A

1. No one is a strang-er here, ev-'ry-one be-longs.
2. We are now a fam-i-ly of which the Lord is head.

Bb   C7   F   Dm   Gm7   Csus C

Find-ing our for-give-ness here, we in turn for-give all wrongs.
Through un-seen, he meets us here in the break-ing of the bread.

126. COME, SHARE THE LORD

Eat This Bread and Never Hunger

Mark 10:46–52; John 4:5–42; 11:1–45
Communion

Words and Music by
Daniel Charles Damon

Eat this bread and nev-er hun-ger;
Drink this cup and nev-er thirst. Christ in-
vites us to the ta-ble where the last be-come the first.

1. Ask-ing for a cup of wa-ter, Je-sus
2. Walk-ing down a des-ert high-way, Je-sus
3. Weep-ing for his friend at grave-side, Je-sus

touched for-bid-den ground; and the wo-man,
healed a man born blind; soon the man be-
felt the pain of death; yet he knew God's

with a ques-tion, told the world what she had found.
came a wit-ness, to the truth we seek and find.
power to wak-en, liv-ing wa-ter, liv-ing breath.

127. EAT THIS BREAD AND NEVER HUNGER

I Am the Bread of Life

John 6:35, 51, 54
Communion

Words adapt. S. Suzanne Toolan
Music by S. Suzanne Toolan

	A	F#m	A/C#
1.	"I am the bread of	life.	You who
2.	"The bread that I will	give	is my
3.	"Un - less ____ you ___	eat	of the
4.	"I am the res - ur - rec - tion,		
5.	Yes, Lord, ____ I be - lieve	that	

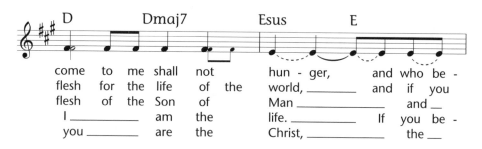

	D	Dmaj7	Esus	E
	come to me shall not	hun - ger,	and who be -	
	flesh for the life of the	world, ____	and if you	
	flesh of the Son of	Man ____	and _	
	I ____ am the	life. ____	If you be -	
	you ____ are the	Christ, ____	the _	

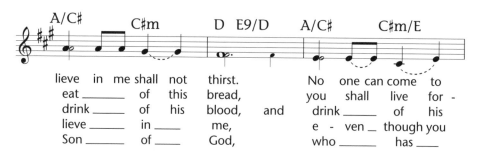

	A/C#	C#m	D E9/D	A/C#	C#m/E
	lieve in me shall not	thirst.	No one can come to		
	eat ____ of this	bread,	you shall live for -		
	drink ____ of his	blood, and	drink ____ of his		
	lieve ____ in ____	me,	e - ven _ though you		
	Son ____ of ____	God,	who ____ has ___		

	F#m	Amaj7	Bm7	E
	me	un - less the	Fa - ther beck - ons."	
	ev - er,	you shall	live for - ev - er."	
	blood,	you shall	not have life with - in you."	
	die, ____	you shall	live for - ev - er."	
	come	in - to ____	the ___ world.	

128. I AM THE BREAD OF LIFE

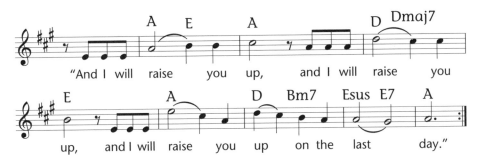

"And I will raise you up, and I will raise you up, and I will raise you up on the last day."

In the Singing

Communion

Words by Shirley Erena Murray
Music by Carlton R. Young

1. In the sing - ing, in the si - lence, in the hands ex - pec - tant, o - pen, in the bless - ing, in the break - ing, in the Pres - ence at this ta - ble—
2. In the ques - tion, in the an - swer, in the mo - ment of ac - cep - tance, in the heart's cry, in the heal - ing, in the cir - cle of your peo - ple—

Je - sus Christ, Je - sus Christ, be the wine of grace:

Je - sus Christ, Je - sus Christ, be the bread of peace.

One Bread, One Body

John 17:13–23
Communion

Words and Music by
John Foley, S.J.

Partakers of the Holy Food

Communion

Words and Music by
Kevin Boyd

1. Par - tak - ers of the Ho - ly Food,
2. Re - ceiv - ers of the Bread and Wine,

Our spir - its filled, our lives re - newed. We will
We are the branch - es, Christ the vine.

wor - ship God as One. Might-y things our Lord has

done! Christ was brok - en, Christ was raised!

We give our lives in love and praise.

We Remember You

Luke 22:14–20; 1 Cor. 11:23–26; Rev. 5:12–14
Communion

Words and Music by
Walt Harrah

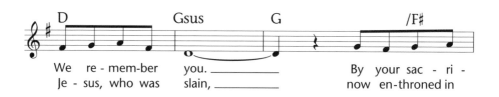

1. We re-mem-ber you, _____
2. Pre-cious ris-en Lamb, _____

We re-mem-ber you. _____ By your sac-ri-
Je-sus, who was slain, _____ now en-throned in

fice of love all glo-ry now is
glo - ry, for-ev-er you will

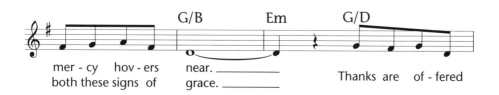

due. At this ta-ble here _____
reign. Glad-ly we em-brace _____

mer-cy hov-ers near. _____ Thanks are of-fered
both these signs of grace. _____

up.   In this bread and   cup   we   re - mem - ber

you. _____   Thanks are   of - fered   up.

In   this bread and   cup   we   re - mem - ber   you.

132. WE REMEMBER YOU

Come, Holy Spirit

Rom. 8:22–27
Liturgical Year/Spirit/Pentecost

Words and Music by
The Iona Community

Come, Ho - ly Spir - it,

grac - ious heaven - ly dove; come, fire of

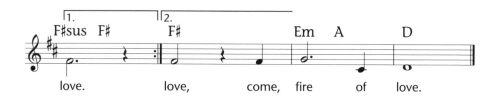

love. love, come, fire of love.

133. COME, HOLY SPIRIT

As You Travel from This Place

Departing/Benediction

Words and Music by
Jim Strathdee

As you trav-el from this place our love is

with you, When you jour-ney near at hand or far a-

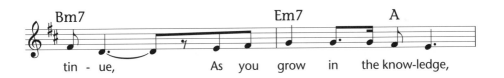

broad. All the life we've shared to-geth-er will con-

tin-ue, As you grow in the know-ledge,

learn of the wis-dom, and live in the spir-it of our God.

Dance with the Spirit

Departing

Words and Music by
Jim Strathdee

135. DANCE WITH THE SPIRIT

Freely, Freely

Matt. 10:8b
Departing/Forgiveness/Offering

Music by
Carol Owens

1. God for - gave my sin in Je - sus'
2. All __ pow'r is giv'n in Je - sus'

name. I've been born a - gain in Je - sus'
name, in __ earth and heav'n in Je - sus'

name. And in Je - sus' name I come to
name. And in Je - sus' name I come to

you to share his love as he told me to.
you to share his pow'r as he told me to.

He said, "Free - ly, free - ly, you have re - ceived,

free - ly, free - ly give. Go in my name, and be -

cause you be - lieve, oth - ers will know that I live."

No One Will Ever Be the Same

Departing

Words and Music by
The Iona Community
Tune: *Roystonhill* (JLB)

1. We're going to shine like the sun in the
2. We're going to learn from the poor in the
3. We're going to walk with the weak in the
4. We're going to drink new __ wine in the
5. And _____ it all starts __ now in the

King-dom of Heav - en, shine like the sun in the
King-dom of Heav - en, learn from the poor in the
King-dom of Heav - en, walk with the weak in the
King-dom of Heav - en, drink new __ wine in the
King-dom of Heav - en, all starts now in the

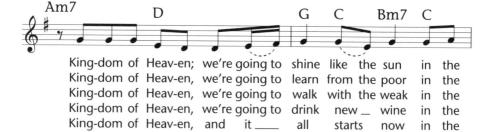

King-dom of Heav-en; we're going to shine like the sun in the
King-dom of Heav-en, we're going to learn from the poor in the
King-dom of Heav-en, we're going to walk with the weak in the
King-dom of Heav-en, we're going to drink new __ wine in the
King-dom of Heav-en, and it __ all starts now in the

King-dom of Heav - en and no one will ev - er be the same.
King-dom of Heav - en and no one will ev - er be the same.
King-dom of Heav - en and no one will ev - er be the same.
King-dom of Heav - en and no one will ev - er be the same.
King-dom of Heav - en and no one will ev - er be the same.

137. NO ONE WILL EVER BE THE SAME

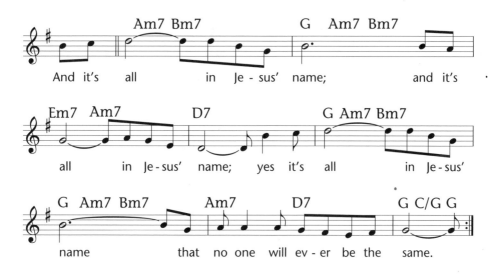

And it's all in Je - sus' name; and it's

all in Je - sus' name; yes it's all in Je - sus'

name that no one will ev - er be the same.

Go with God

Rom. 8:14
Departing/Benediction

Words and Music by
Isaiah Jones, Jr.

Go with God. Go with God. As you

leave this place, go with God. God will di -

rect your way, God will light ev - 'ry day.

As you leave this place, go with God.

The Tools of the Trade

Eph. 6:11–20
Departing

Words and Music by
Kinley Lange

G A D F#m

1. All a - round us there is beau-ty and
2. As a car - pen - ter con - sid - ers the

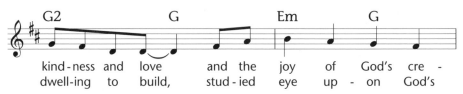

G2 G Em G

kind - ness and love and the joy of God's cre -
dwell-ing to build, stud - ied eye up - on God's

D/A A D F#m

a - tion. There is al - so des - pair and de -
plan, she takes cour-age and pride in the

G2 G Em G

cep - tion and pain and an ar - my of temp -
tools at her side and the strength in her own

D/A A G A/G

ta - tion. How shall we live as
hands. _____ How will she make a

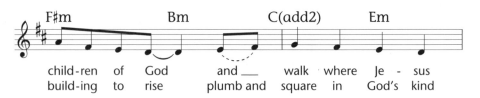

F#m Bm C(add2) Em

child-ren of God and __ walk where Je - sus
build-ing to rise plumb and square in God's kind

139. THE TOOLS OF THE TRADE

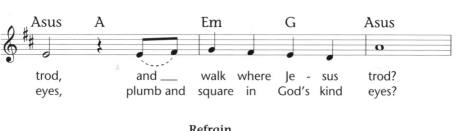
trod,   and ___ walk where Je - sus trod?
eyes,   plumb and square in God's kind eyes?

Refrain

Put   on   the   whole   ar - mor, the word of the Lord.

Step   out   in   faith   and   be   not   a - fraid. ___

Take time to   pray   and lis - ten   and   sing a new song.

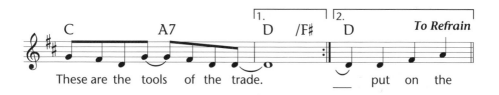
These are   the   tools   of   the   trade. ___

These are the tools of the trade.   ___ put   on   the

139. THE TOOLS OF THE TRADE

God's Love Made Visible

John 1:1–14; 3:16
Liturgical Year/Advent

Words by Iola Brubeck, 1975
Music by Dave Brubeck, 1975

1. God's love made vis - i - ble! In - com - pre - hen - si - ble!
2. God gave his Son to us to dwell as one of us,

He is in - vin - ci - ble! His love shall reign!
His bless - ing un - to us! His love shall reign!

From love so boun - ti - ful, bless - ings un - count - a - ble,
To Him all hon - or bring, heav - en and earth will sing,

make death sur - mount - a - ble! His love shall reign!
prais - ing our Lord and King! His love shall reign!

Joy - ful - ly pray for peace and good will.
O - pen all doors this day of his birth,

All of our yearn - ing he will ful - fill.
all of good will in - her - it the earth.

Live in a lov - ing way. Praise him for ev - 'ry day.
His star will al - ways be guid - ing hu - man - i - ty

O - pen your hearts and pray. His love shall reign!
through-out e - ter - ni - ty! His love shall reign!

140. GOD'S LOVE MADE VISIBLE

There Is a Longing

Isa. 11:1–10; Rom. 15:12
Liturgical Year/Advent

Words and Music by
Anne Quigley

There is a long-ing in our hearts, O Lord, for
you to re-veal your-self to us. _____ There is a
long-ing in our hearts for love we on-ly find in you, our God.

1. For jus - tice, for free - dom, for
2. For wis - dom, for cour - age, for
3. For heal - ing, for whole - ness, for
4. Lord save us, take pit - y, light

mer - cy: hear our prayer. __ In sor - row,
com - fort: hear our prayer. __ In weak - ness,
new life: hear our prayer. __ In sick - ness,
in our dark - ness. _____ We call you,

in grief: be near, hear our prayer, O God.
in fear:
in death:
we wait:

141.   THERE IS A LONGING

Soon and Very Soon

Rev. 22:20
Liturgical Year/Funeral/Advent

Words and Music by
Andraé Crouch

1. Soon and ver - y soon, we are going to see the King.
2. No more cry-ing there, we are going to see the King.
3. No more dy-ing there, we are going to see the King.

Soon and ver - y soon, we are going to see the King.
No more cry - ing there, we are going to see the King.
No more dy - ing there, we are going to see the King.

Soon and ver - y soon, we are going to see the King.
No more cry - ing there, we are going to see the King.
No more dy - ing there, we are going to see the King.

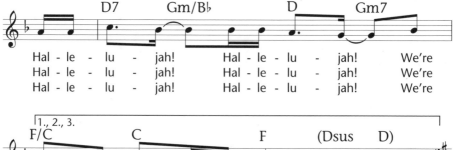

Hal - le - lu - jah! Hal - le - lu - jah! We're
Hal - le - lu - jah! Hal - le - lu - jah! We're
Hal - le - lu - jah! Hal - le - lu - jah! We're

1., 2., 3.

going to see the King!
going to see the King!
going to see the King!

142. SOON AND VERY SOON

4. Soon and ver - y soon, we are going to see the King.

Soon and ver - y soon, we are going to see the King.

Soon and ver - y soon, we are going to see the King.

Hal-le - lu - jah! Hal-le-lu - jah! We're going to see the King.

Hal-le - lu - jah! Hal-le-lu - jah! We're going to see the King.

Hal-le - lu - jah! Hal-le-lu - jah! We're going to see the

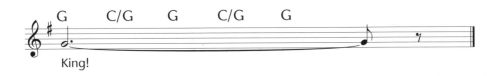

King!

142. SOON AND VERY SOON

Emmanuel, Emmanuel

Matt. 1:18–25
Liturgical Year/Advent

Words and Music by
Bob McGee

Em-man - u - el, Em-man - u - el, his name is called Em - man - u - el. God with us, re - vealed in us, his name is called Em - man - u - el.

I Am the Light of the World

John 8:12
Liturgical Year/Christmas/Justice

Words and Music by
Jim Strathdee

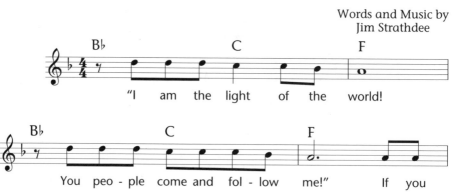

"I am the light of the world! You peo - ple come and fol - low me!" If you

follow and love you'll learn the mystery of
what you were meant to do and be.

1. When the song of the angels is ____ stilled, when the
2. To find ____ the lost and lonely one, _____ to
3. To free ____ the prisoner from all chains, ____ to
4. To bring hope ____ to every task you do, _____ to

star in the sky ____ is ____ gone, when the
heal ____ the broken soul with love, _____ to
make ____ the powerful ____ care, _____ to
dance at a ba - by's new birth, _____ to

kings ____ and the shepherds have found their way home, the
feed the hungry children with warmth and good food, to
re - build the nations with strength of good will, to
make ____ music in ____ an old person's heart, and

work ____ of ____ Christmas is be - gun:
feel the earth be - low, the sky a - bove!
see ____ God's ____ children every - where!
sing ____ to the colors of the earth!

144. I AM THE LIGHT OF THE WORLD

Hosanna

Mark 11:1–11
Liturgical Year/Palm Sunday/Christ the King

Words and Music by
Carl Tuttle

145. HOSANNA

Jesus Took a Towel

John 13:3–10
Liturgical Year/Footwashing/Maundy Thursday

Words and Music by
Chrysogonus Waddell, OCSO, 1968

Je-sus took a tow-el and he gird-ed him-self, then he washed my feet, yes, he washed my feet. Je-sus took a ba-sin and he knelt him-self down, and he washed, yes he washed my feet.

1. The heav-ens are the Lord's, and the earth is his, the clouds are his char-iot, ___ glo-ry his cloak. He made ___ the moun-tains, set the lim-its of the sea, and he stooped and washed my feet. ___

2. The hour had ___ come, ___ the feast was near; ___ Je-sus loved his own, loved them to the end. O Lord, let me see, ___ let me un-der-stand why you stooped and washed my feet.

146. JESUS TOOK A TOWEL

Come and See

Matt. 27:27–44; Mark 15:16–32; Luke 23:8–11, 35–39; John 19:5, 17
Liturgical Year/Good Friday

Words and Music by
Graham Kendrick

1. Come and see, come and see, come and
2. Come and weep, come and mourn for your
3. Man of heav'n, born to earth to re -

see the King of love, see the pur - ple robe and
sin that pierced him there so much deep - er than the
store us to your heav'n, here we bow in awe be -

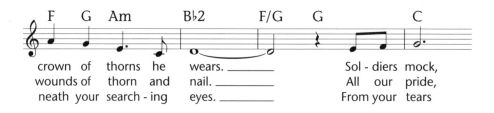

crown of thorns he wears. _____ Sol - diers mock,
wounds of thorn and nail. _____ All our pride,
neath your search - ing eyes. _____ From your tears

ru - lers sneer, as he lifts the cru - el cross,
all our greed, all our fall - en - ness and shame,
comes our joy. From your death our life shall spring.

lone and friend-less now, he climbs to - wards the hill. _____
and the Lord has laid the pun - ish - ment on him. _____
By your re - sur - rec - tion pow - er we shall rise. _____

147. COME AND SEE

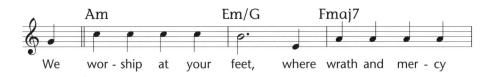

We wor-ship at your feet, where wrath and mer-cy

meet, and a guilt-y world is washed by love's pure

stream. _____ For us he was made sin, oh,

help me take it in. Deep wounds of love cry

out, "Fa-ther for-give." _____ I wor-ship, I

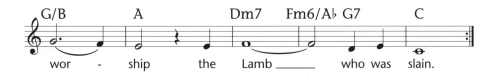

wor - ship the Lamb _____ who was slain.

147. COME AND SEE

Glory

Luke 2:13–14; John 1:10, 29, 36
Liturgical Year/Easter

Words and Music by
Danny Daniels

148. GLORY

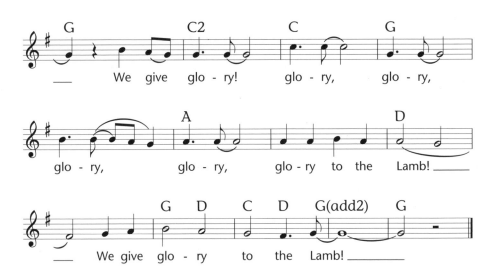

We give glo - ry! glo - ry, glo - ry,

glo - ry, glo - ry, glo - ry to the Lamb! ____

We give glo - ry to the Lamb! ____

148. GLORY

You Are Mighty

Matt. 28:1–20; Mark 16:1–6; Luke 24:1–9, 34; John 20:1–19
Liturgical Year/Easter

Words and Music by
Craig Musseau

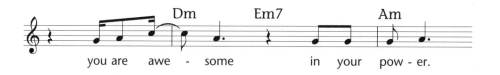

You are might - y, you are ho - ly,

you are awe - some in your pow - er.

You have ris - en, you have con - quered, you have beat -

(repeat first time only)

- en the power of death.

Hal - le - lu - jah, we will re - joice.

Hal - le - lu - jah, we will re -

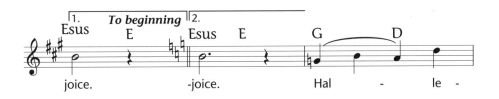

149. YOU ARE MIGHTY

He Is Lord

Phil. 2:10–11
Liturgical Year/Easter

Author/Composer unknown

1. He is Lord, he is Lord!

He is ris - en from the dead, and he is Lord!

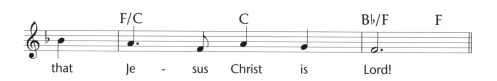

Ev - 'ry knee shall bow, ev - 'ry tongue con - fess

that Je - sus Christ is Lord!

2. He is love, he is love!

He has shown us by his life that he is love!

All his peo - ple sing with one voice of joy

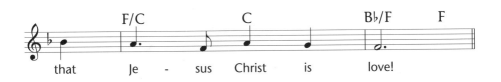

that Je - sus Christ is love!

3. He is life, he is life!

He has died to set us free and he is life!

And he calls us all to live ev - er - more,

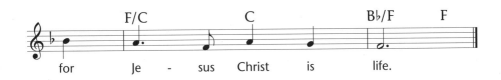

for Je - sus Christ is life.

Come, Spirit, Come

John 16:12–15
Liturgical Year/Pentecost

Words and Music by
Walt Harrah

Come, Ho - ly Spir - it, dwell here a -

mong us. We need your pow - er,

your heal - ing grace. Show us your fa - vor,

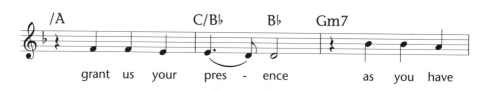

grant us your pres - ence as you have

prom - ised. Come, Spir - it, come. come.

Come, rush - ing wind, come ho - ly fire,

here and now de - scend. O breath of God, O

per - fect peace, re - vive us once a - gain. ___

come. As you have prom - ised,

come, Spir - it, come.

151. COME, SPIRIT, COME

Topical Index

Index of Authors, Composers, and Arrangers

Index of Titles